One REMF's Tour of Duty in Vietnam

A Memoir

by

James Paul Lott

One REMF's Tour of Duty in Vietnam

A Memoir

by

James Paul Lott

© 2018 by James Paul Lott. All rights reserved. No part of this book may be reproduced or transmitted in any form or by any means, electronic, mechanical, photocopying, recording, or otherwise, without the express written permission of the author.

ISBN-13: 9781797950358 (print)

To My Wife, Patty

Prologue: Reflections on My Year in Vietnam

I want others to know what I experienced as a United States Army ground soldier in the Vietnam War. There are many published and existing accounts of soldiers who served in Vietnam. My account is honest and so truthful that some of the content may be hard to read by dear, kind, innocent women and children. That being said, I want others to read it, including my own children and grandchildren. Since leaving, I have thought about Vietnam every day and every night of my life. The mental flashbacks are difficult to control whether being awake or asleep.

I would not take a million dollars for my memories of Vietnam—or do it again for a million dollars. I honestly never thought I would ever write a book about the war, but I find it is a lot easier to write about it than talk about it in person. Civilians just don't understand, and neither do some veterans. There have been times when someone, even Vietnam vets, asked me what my job was. When I said truck driver, they would say, "Oh, you had it made." They just didn't know. Based on where you were, what your job was, what kind of unit you were with, and when you were in Vietnam, everyone has a different story and memory of Vietnam. This book has been my story and my experiences. Hopefully this gives anyone who reads it a realistic perspective of my war.

At times, I truly loved and enjoyed what I did and would not have traded the experience, the people I served with, and the many friends I had for anything. Looking back, I cannot help but smile when I think about all the wonderful experiences I had and all the truly embarrassing, immature things we did. It was the times, the circumstances, and the behavior—which can be expected of those eighteen to twenty years old. But on the other hand, Vietnam was truly a hellish place to be. Regardless of where you were, it was grueling, brutal, savage, hot, dirty, and dangerous for almost everyone. To be truthful, on many occasions I was scared by what I saw and what was happening around me.

For me, I feel very lucky to be alive today and to have served my country and, in my mind, to have survived the greatest, most exciting, and most terrified year of my life. I am deeply appreciative of all the help I have received from everyone who has helped with the writing of this book. God bless my friends from so many years ago and all the other vets of all wars who gave their best and suffer mentally or physically.

This writing is dedicated to my wife for putting up with me for over forty years. I love you.

CHAPTER

1

Growing Up in a Small Town

On the morning of September 7, 1969, the pilot came on the air to let us know where we were and to give the current weather and ground conditions just prior to landing. Depending on how you viewed it, the guy had a real sense of humor. He announced that the ground conditions consisted of "light to scattered automatic weapons fire" and a few other things I don't remember. It was designed to scare the crap out of you. This prepared us for the worst.

Before I go on about my tour of duty in Vietnam, I should tell about how I got here. I was born on March 2, 1949, in a small town of about three thousand souls called Hominy, Oklahoma. It is about twenty-five miles north of Tulsa, Oklahoma. Hominy was, at one time, a part of the Cherokee Reservation in Indian Territory. However, there were Osage Indians living in this area in the 1800s. In 1872, the government bought land from the Cherokee to move the Osage Tribe into Indian Territory. Hominy was one of the three original districts settled by the Osages. Little did anyone know, this piece of land on the Osage Reservation was abundant in oil. It soon made them the richest tribe in the United States. With its arrival in 1903, the railroad played a key part in the growth of Hominy. In 1906, the reservation land became Osage County with statehood soon after in 1907. Oil played a major part in the development of Hominy. Today, ranching and oil continue to be the main industries located in the town.

The Hominy Indians were a professional American football team in Hominy during the 1920s and 1930s. The Indians were an all Native American team, with players from twenty-two different tribes. They accomplished a twenty-eight-game winning streak during their time of play. The Hominy Indians quickly rose to fame as they defeated other teams throughout the country. The Indians had never been defeated or even tied as they entered into the biggest game of their existence. On December 26, 1927, the Hominy Indians had a chance to play the current world champions, the New York Giants. Three weeks after the Giants defeated the New York Rangers for the national title, they traveled to Oklahoma to face the dominating Hominy Indians. The Indians defeated the Giants 13–6 in front of what was said to be about two thousand fans.

My father and mother, Russell and Ora Lee Lott, named me James Paul Lott. I was the tenth child born into their family. There were six boys and four girls. My siblings' names are Viola, JT, Dorothy, Leona, Billy, Wanda, Carl, Charles, and Richard. My mother was having babies for twenty years, from July 1929 until March 1949. Can you imagine all of the diapers? The oldest child, Viola, had gotten married before I was born. The second-oldest child, JT, got married soon after I was born. While I was growing up, there were at least eight of us children in the house—three girls and five boys.

When I was six months old, my mother and father got a divorce. My mother said my father liked to drink and stay out all night and on weekends. She said he would tell her she could go with him but she couldn't because she had to take care of the children. I never knew what a father was growing up. I was twenty-five years old when I first met my father. After my father left, my mother had to do whatever she could to put food on the table because my father did nothing to help her out. She would babysit other people's children while taking care of her own at the same time. She would also do other people's laundry and ironing. She also cleaned their houses.

On the weekends during cotton season, she would pick cotton and get paid two cents a pound. It was a very hot and dirty job. If a person was very fast, they could make anywhere from $5.00 to $7.00 a day. They would work from sunrise to sunset. On Fridays and Saturdays when cotton season was over, she would wash dishes at the Hominy Sale Barn. It was a place where they sold cows, horses, and pigs. She would make about $10.00 to $12.00 all day from 7:00 am until 5.00 pm. After that, she would still go home and fix all the children something to eat. Looking back on it now, I don't know how she did it all, but I do know she did it for her children. My mother never remarried. I never even saw her with another man. She passed away in April of 2000 at the age of eighty-nine. She was a fine and beautiful woman and mother to us and I miss her very much.

I guess you could say we were poor, but I didn't know it at the time. One Sunday night just a few days before Christmas when I was about five or six years old, we returned home from church and under the small Christmas tree that my older brother cut down from the nearby hill were the most gifts I had ever seen. The people from church had gotten them for us kids, knowing that my mother had no money to buy us anything. To this day, that was the best Christmas I've ever had. There were other times when the people from church did it again, but that one time has always been very special to me.

One cold January, we got about two feet of snow. We had no car and my mother never learned how to drive. We had no way to get to the grocery store to

The family, from youngest on the left to the oldest, taken in the late '80s: Paul, Richard, twins Charles and Carl, Wanda, Billie, Leona, Dorothy, JT, then Fatty (Viola). Mom, Ora Lott, is in the front. She was also a twin (Ora and Nora).

buy food. Once again, the people from our church came by with something they had bought or cooked. This happened every day for a week. One day I walked in on my mother crying. I asked her what she was crying about, and she said that she was thanking God for answering her prayers. I often think about that church, those people, and the small town I called home. Growing up in a small town like Hominy, everyone knew everyone. I would not trade my experience growing up there for anything. I had a lot of good times and bad times, as anyone does in life. Looking back on it now, there were more good than bad.

When I was about ten years old, I was walking home from school and our neighbor, Mr. Smith, was putting gas in his lawn mower. He and his wife were very nice people. Every time I would pass his house, he would ask how I was doing. On this particular summer day, he stopped me and asked if I would like to mow his lawn. He said he would pay me $2.00 and I could even use his mower. I was excited because $2.00 was a lot of money back then. Without hesitation, I told him I would do it but would also have to ask my mother for permission. He told me to go home and ask her and that if it was fine by her, to return at 8:00 am that following day. He knew it was going to be Saturday and I would not be in school. My mother gave me her permission, so I was at Mr. Smith's that next morning at 8:00 am sharp. I had never used a lawn mower before so he taught me how it worked, how to take care of it, and how to put gas and oil in it. He also walked me around the yard showing me what to mow and what not to mow. In the end, it would take me about two hours to mow their lawn. After I was done, he had a large glass of iced tea waiting for me and the $2.00 I had earned. He told me I did a very good job and asked if I would come back the following Saturday, which I did.

That next Monday after school, I was walking by Mr. Smith's house again and I noticed that he was working on something in his small shop by the house. He was fixing up his old mower for someone because he just bought himself a new one. For the next four days on my walks home, he would be in his shop working on that old mower. When Saturday morning came, I showed up at 8:00 am to mow his yard. Mr. Smith came outside and went to his shop and brought out the old mower he was working on. He repainted it, replaced the cutting blades, and put on a new starter rope. It looked nearly new now. He told me to use the old mower and to see how it worked. After mowing the yard, Mrs. Smith came out with a big glass of iced tea and Mr. Smith gave me the $2.00. He asked what I was going to buy with the money I was making. I told him I was saving up to buy a new mower so I could mow more yards around town. Before I could start walking back home, he told me to take the old mower and mow all the yards I could with it. He told me that he was fixing it up for me, that it was a gift from him and his wife. I was speechless. For the next two years, I mowed yards until the mower quit working. From the time that Mr. Smith gave me that old mower until he passed away a few years later, I would only take a big glass of iced tea for mowing his yard on those Saturdays. Whenever I return to Hominy from time to time, I always go by his old house and remember the good times I had and that old mower he gave me.

From then on, I had a lot of different jobs growing up. I once worked in a hay field, picked cotton, and had a newspaper route after school. I also worked at a grocery store. The best job I had was at the Chevy dealership, though. My best friend Gary had gotten a job there and he said I should go down and ask for one as well. They were looking for another kid to wash cars and help clean up around the dealership. After school one day, I went down there and talked to Mr. James, the owner. He said I could work part time after school and on Saturdays for $1.25 an hour. Gary and I had a lot of fun working there. In the back of the dealership, there was a place to wash and detail the vehicles. During the summer when it was hot, we would wash the vehicles and have water fights to keep cool. We got more water on ourselves than the cars most of the time.

In 1965, I turned sixteen and decided to take my driving test. I took my test with my brother's 1954 Chevy and passed on the first try. One day when I got to work, there was a 1955 Chevy two-door on the car lot. Someone had traded it in for a new car. As I went over to check it out, Mr. James came walking up and said to get it washed and waxed because it would sell fast. As I was driving it to the back of the shop to clean it up, I decided to see how much power it had. I pushed the gas pedal all the way down and almost lost control of it. At the time, I had never driven a car with that much power before. The motor was a 327. Someone had taken out the old 265 and replaced it with the much bigger and more powerful 327. I fell in love with that car right then and there. I asked Mr. James how much he was going to sell it for. $175.00 was going to be the asking price, but he would take $150.00 from me since I was doing a good job for him so far. No more walking for me. I drove it home that day.

On my way home that day, I stopped to put gas in it. It was $.29 a gallon. A high price for gas, I thought to myself. I had a lot of good times in that car. My first kiss was in that car. In those days, if you had a hot car, all the girls would ask you for a ride. No problem, in my eyes. There was this one girl I liked a lot, Paula. The song "Hey, Hey, Paula" became our song. All the kids had an eight-track tape player in their cars, so I soon followed suit and bought and installed one in that old Chevy of mine. Paula and I would play that song over and over. Some nights we would drive out to Hominy Lake and park the car on this hill that overlooked the lake. We would talk and listen to songs on the eight-track tape player. It seemed like we always ended up in the back seat of the car. Often, we would go to the drive-in show in Tulsa. Most of the time, I wouldn't be able to tell you what show was playing because we would be in the back seat having a good time of our own, if you know what I mean.

One night I went to pick Paula up at her house and as she got into the car, I could tell something was on her mind. She was hardly saying a word to me. I asked if something was wrong, but all she would do was just sit there and not say a word. I drove out to the lake and parked the car. We sat there for a long time before Paula told me that she had something to say. I will never forget those two words: "I'm pregnant." I didn't know what to say.

After a few moments of silence, I said without thinking, "How did that happen?"

Silly me.

Slyly she said, "One too many times in the back seat."

Even though I loved her, I was planning on waiting to get married until I got a better-paying job. We talked hour after hour about everything from where we would live to how we could pay for raising a child. We even talked about baby names and possible wedding dates. By the time she told me, she had already gone to the doctor once. The baby was to be due in late June or early July. We set a wedding date for January of 1968.

After we got married, we were going to move into her parents' apartment they had over their garage. It was small and had one bedroom. By this time, we were both out of school. I started looking for a better-paying job but they were hard to come by in a small town. I was working more hours at the dealership, but I knew it would not be enough to take care of a wife, a new baby, bills, and food. One night I was watching the news on our small black-and-white television. They were talking about a place overseas that was in Southeast Asia. They were talking about people getting killed. I didn't pay too much attention to it at the time, but I sure would later on. There was a lot of talk about the Army and the draft. The news was talking about boys between the ages of eighteen and nineteen being drafted.

CHAPTER
2

Uncle Sam Wants You

Near the end of 1967, Paula was getting a little bigger and I was working more hours. We were trying to save money to pay for the hospital bills that were going to be coming after the birth. One day, the Hominy newspaper had a story about a boy I had grown up with and how he died in this place called Vietnam. That was the first time I had ever heard of Vietnam. After that, the television news was talking about Vietnam and showing pictures of men fighting in the jungle. Instead of men, I should say boys. The average age of the soldiers in Vietnam was nineteen years old, according to government statistics. Too young to buy and drink beer or alcohol legally, too young to register to vote, but old enough to carry a rifle and kill someone on foreign land.

My brother Richard, who is two years older than me, was going to sign up for the Army. Why? I don't know. He went to take his physical, but failed it because of a bad heart. As a result, Uncle Sam said goodbye to him. In October of 1967, my brother Carl, four years my senior, received his letter from the draft board. The letter stated that he was getting an all-expenses-paid trip to a tropical jungle in Southeast Asia. That's how Carl tells it these days, anyways. On October 10, 1967, Carl's twin, Charles, and I pulled up in front of the main Post Office and Federal Building in Tulsa, Oklahoma, to drop Carl off to catch a bus down to Oklahoma City. After a few short goodbyes, he boarded at 6:00 am. On the drive home, I kept thinking of the television news and the pictures of Vietnam they kept showing. It left me hoping that Carl would be sent to a safe place in Vietnam, if there was such a place in a war zone. The reason Charles didn't get a letter from the draft board was because he had joined the Army Reserve the month before. Why Carl didn't do that, I don't know.

Carl was stationed at Fort Polk, Louisiana, for eight weeks of Basic Infantry Training and then eight weeks of Advanced Infantry Training (AIT). One day we got a letter from Carl saying that he would be home in ten days for a two-week leave. At the end of his letter he said that he was having all kinds of fun and wished that we were there with him. Of course he added "not really" at the end.

When we picked him up at the bus station for his two-week leave, I asked him how he liked the Army. He said he didn't like it very much. He was home for two weeks before being sent to Fort Lewis, Washington, before going to Vietnam.

One night in January, I was sitting in front of the little black-and-white television watching the news broadcast hoping to see Carl or anything about Vietnam. The Tet Offensive had begun in Vietnam. Tet is the Lunar New Year for the Vietnamese people. The enemy—which included the Viet Cong and North Vietnamese Regular Army, or troops in uniform—had brought the war from the jungles and small villages and hamlets into the large cities in South Vietnam. At the time, the capital of South Vietnam was Saigon. In Saigon, the enemy was referred to as "Charlie" by the United States troops. Charlie attacked the U.S. Embassy, the television station, and the radio station "for effect." They did this to demonstrate that they could and would ratchet up the war on their terms. Tet of 1968 became the turning point of the war. U.S. ground troops in January 1968 were numbering 525,000 and the strength peaked in February 1968 at 540,000. It was said to never get any larger than that. 1968 was also shaping up to be the bloodiest year of the Vietnam War so far. It looked as if the war was spreading too, towards Cambodia, Laos, and even super-power nations such as China and Russia. They both had warhead missiles available to use. It was getting damn scary watching network television.

On March 2, 1968, I turned nineteen years old: just the right time and age for the draft. Around that same time, I received my first letter from my brother Carl. He said this was the first time he has had the chance to write home since being in Vietnam. He also said it was one place that nobody should want to be. He told me to do whatever it took to stay away from that place. He said that they just returned from a seven-day search-and-destroy mission walking through the jungle. They were in the central highlands, near the "A Shau Valley," with the 101st Airborne Division, Infantry. He said they would be taken out on helicopters and dropped off somewhere so they could walk until dark to set up an ambush on the Viet Cong. The weight of their packs was around sixty pounds. They also added four canteens of water, food, extra ammo for their M-60 machine gun, and a canvas belt that holds twenty clips of ammo for the M-16 in another rucksack. He said their backs and shoulders would ache with pain. They had to carry that, walk, and keep their eyes open for any Viet Cong snipers in the area.

He said the temperature during the day in Vietnam was always up in the high nineties. This only made the going that much more difficult in the jungle. The humidity and sweat made it even worse. Every time they stopped to rest or wade through water to cross streams or creeks, they had to check for leeches that would attach to their bodies and suck their blood for a free meal. He said on more than one occasion, he would have a dozen or so attached to his legs and arms. Sticking the end of a lit cigarette or the tip of a lit match on one would make it fall off. One guy, however, had a serious problem one morning. After sleeping on the jungle ground, he woke up to go take a piss. He about fainted after finding several large leeches on his balls and several more attached to his manhood. While everyone else was laughing, deep down they were praying it would not happen to any of them.

Carl went on, saying that their last night in the jungle, around 2:00 am, some Viet Cong, or VC, walked up on their ambush and all hell broke loose. He said they killed four VC without any of their own being killed or wounded. He told me that the reason he's writing and telling me this is so that I understood how bad it was over there. He said if I were to sign up, they would station me someplace besides Vietnam because the Army would not send two brothers to a war zone at the same time. He did not want me over in Vietnam because it was a "hell hole." Towards the end of his letter, he told me he had to go and clean his weapons and get his gear ready because they would be going back out on another search-and-destroy mission at first light. He told me to tell everyone hello and said he would write more when and if he had the time. He also advised me to go talk to an Army recruiter.

After reading his letter, I was not ashamed to admit that I was a little worried because I had a lot to think about. I now had a wife to care for and, soon, a new baby. For the next month, all I could think about was my letter from Carl. There was more and more news on the television about the war in Vietnam. It seemed like everywhere you went, people would be talking about the war in Southeast Asia and all the boys getting killed. Every day the newspaper had a story about some boy being killed or wounded in Vietnam. They said by the end of 1967, there had been 15,979 Americans killed in action there.

By the end of March, I received my second letter from now-Specialist E-4 Carl Lott. He said they had just returned to their base camp for a five-day rest. For the past two weeks, day and night, they had been walking in triple-canopy jungle. He said during the day, the canopy was so thick the sunlight could not get through. He described it as "walking at night." They would sleep, eat, and shit in the jungle. The days were very hot and the nights very cold. In the past two weeks, they had five Wounded in Action (WIA) and two Killed in Action (KIA). He said the jungle was so thick and tangled with vines that they would reach up and grab their legs and trip them every other step they took. It made walking difficult and dangerous. They called them "wait a minute vines" because you had to stop and wait a minute to get free of them. He reminded me of how bad of a place Vietnam was and asked if I talked to an Army recruiter yet. He said for the past two days, he'd done nothing but catch up on sleep because when they're "in the bush," they're always on alert for the VC. He said he'd been able to relax and catch up on sleep and didn't have to do any bullshit jobs, such as guard duty or extra duty, because all of that was left to the "REMF guys." He went on to describe REMF as a term used by infantry guys to describe those in cushy jobs in the rear. It is short for Rear Echelon Mother Fucker. The guys that stay in base camps and never leave are REMF guys. They're also known as the "guys in the rear with the gear."

Yet again after reading Carl's letter, I could hardly sleep because of all the thinking I had to do. Paula and I talked about it almost every night. On the first of April, Paula and I went to talk to the Army recruiter in Tulsa. The recruiter we spoke to was a sergeant first class, E-7 pay grade. He said he had been in the Army for sixteen years, with four more to go until he was able to retire. He also said that it had been a good career for him. He said that he'd been all over the world, and that Germany was his favorite duty station overall. He had completed two tours of duty in Vietnam from 1965 to 1966 and again from 1967 to 1968. He said it's a bad place to be if you're in the infantry. We talked about Carl being in Vietnam, and he reassured me that as long as he was there, I would not be sent there. He told me that if I was to sign up, I could pick an overseas duty station, such as Germany. Paula would get an allotment of my pay every month, which was comforting. The military would also pay all doctor and medical bills for the two of us and for any and all children to come. He said if I were to wait and not get drafted until after my brother returns from Vietnam, then the Army could send me anywhere, including being a foot soldier in the infantry in Vietnam. After all of the information he gave us, Paula and I went and ate and talked about all that was said at the recruiter's office. We decided it would be best for us if I signed up for the military because of all of the upcoming medical bills and the monthly allotment we would be receiving.

CHAPTER 3

I Am in the Army Now

On April 16, 1968, I signed my name on the dotted line. For the next three years, I would be in Uncle Sam's Army. That next morning, I gathered with other men outside the Federal Building in Tulsa, Oklahoma, to catch a bus for Oklahoma City for induction physicals and oaths of service. It was mind-numbing to think of the future I was about to be facing. My wife was there along with other wives and girlfriends, as well as moms and dads, to see us off. It was 6:00 am when we boarded the bus that would take us to our new life. As we were saying our goodbyes, I was thinking to myself and wondering if I had made the right decision. It was too late to back out now, however. I was thinking if I should tell the bus driver there had been a misunderstanding and that I needed to get off the bus, but before I could say anything, the bus turned off the exit from the turnpike. I was wondering if I was going to be tough enough for what the Army was going to be dishing out. I would soon find out.

We got off the bus and entered the building for the physical examinations and swearing of the oath to defend our country against its enemies. Other buses had deposited many other men, making the total count up to sixty men for that day. We were taken to this large room and stripped down to nothing. So there we were, sixty men all naked. Some were in good athletic condition while others were either overweight and flabby or skinny with different frames. One poor fellow was over six feet tall and must have only weighed about a hundred pounds. Another was so fat he could hardly walk. One had eyeglasses that were as thick as the glass on the bottom of a soda bottle. Despite every possible physical defect, not one man was rejected for induction.

We were all told to stand in a line, with half on one side of the room and the other half on the other side. Sixty naked men facing each other and waiting for the doctor to come by and check us for hernias. I looked across at one point and saw one of the guys with a very large hard-on. Let me tell you, it was larger than average. It was standing at attention all on its own. I'm guessing he had a "piss hard-on," because for the last half hour, he kept asking to go take a piss. For you girls who don't know what a piss hard-on is, it's an erection of the penis that is brought on due to the load pressure present on the man's bladder. The erection is somewhat painful until a man can piss it out, then the erection will be gone. When the doctor came in the room, he was carrying this small footstool with rollers on it. He sat down and rolled it to each man checking for hernias. When he came to the guy with the huge hard-on, he took this small looking washcloth and laid it across the guy's erection.

The doctor asked him, "Are you happy to see me or what?"

The guy said, "No, sir, I just have to piss badly."

Everyone broke out in laughter. The doctor told the guy to go take a piss and to get back as soon as he could.

After the hernia checks, we were told to get dressed and assemble in what appeared to be a courtroom and sit down. An Army officer came in shortly and asked everyone to stand up and raise our right hands to take the oath of service, which we all did. To defend our country against its enemies and promising to lay down our life if need be, so on and so on.

He then said, "Congratulations, you are now all privates in the United States Army."

I was hoping I had done the right thing. We then filed out of the room and boarded buses that drove us to our designated tarmac at the Oklahoma City Will Rogers International Airport. We were ushered by Army officials onto the plane, which already had its motors running, waiting for us to board. It wasn't until we were boarded and in the air that the pilot finally told us where we were going. He said we were flying nonstop to Los Angeles International Airport. From there we were going to be put on buses to our new duty station. We would be there for eight to nine weeks for Basic Training, then we would go to our new duty station, Fort Ord, California.

As fate would have it, Mr. Hard-On got the seat next to me. He turned out to be a really nice guy. He was from the town of Moore, south of Oklahoma City. He had also signed up like myself, but for a different reason. He said he always wanted to be in the military. If he likes it, he said, he would make a career out of it. Mr. Hard-On was named Bob. He was about 5'10" and weighed around two hundred pounds, all muscle. He clearly spent his free time working out. We became good friends. He said he also enlisted so he could be stationed in Germany, where his father had once been. His dad told him of all the good times he had there. I also told him I was hoping for Germany, too. He said it would be nice if we were both stationed together. I agreed. We talked for a long time on the plane, but eventually we both fell asleep because of our early morning. We didn't wake until the pilot came on the air to tell us that we would be landing at LAX in about half an hour.

When we landed, we were taken straight to the two buses where an Army officer stood and waited. Bob asked him if he could go take a piss, and the officer said he would have to wait until we came to our first stop. He said these buses would take us to Fort Ord, and we would be arriving around midnight. It was 7:00 pm when he told us that. We had five hours until our current lifestyle would be changed forever. Bob and I got on the same bus and sat together. We ended up sharing some common interests. We both liked football, fishing, and a hot car. The buses made just two stops on the way, one for gas and one for food. Bob said that just about every time he has a full bladder, he gets a hard-on. He said it's a medical condition. He was afraid that it was going to keep him out of the Army.

About fifteen minutes out of Fort Ord, the bus driver came on the speaker and informed us to stay on the bus until someone tells us to get off. And boy did someone tell us to get off. I'll never forget that someone, too. It would be one of those nights that none of us would ever forget.

CHAPTER 4

Welcome to Fort Ord

Just past midnight, we drove by this very large sign that said "Welcome to Fort Ord, California." In about five minutes' time, the two buses pulled up in front of this very old wooden barracks. Waiting for us outside were about a dozen or so sergeants, or non-commissioned officers (NCOs). The bus doors opened and this huge, fierce, black drill sergeant with a snarl on his face stepped inside the bus. Over six feet tall, he looked like he weighed about three hundred pounds. He looked to be in good enough physical condition to play professional football as a lineman. Without saying a word, he walked to the back of the bus, turned around, and walked back to the front. As he was doing this, everyone was talking, which made it loud on the bus.

He walked over to one guy and pulled him up by a handful of his hair and said, "Who the hell gave you permission to talk, pussy?"

The guy didn't know what to say because he was so frightened. Needless to say, the bus got quiet after that. We could hear the other drill sergeants outside cursing at someone else.

He walked to the bus driver and said: "What in the hell have you done? This is an Army base, not a Marine base. All I see here is a lot of pussies and queers. The Army does not like pussies and queers. Only the Marines like pussies and queers."

About that time, I was starting to really question what I had gotten myself into.

He came over to Bob and myself and said, "What is your name, pussy?"

Bob replied, "Sir, my name is Bob."

The drill sergeant said: "What the fuck did you call me, pussy? When you say anything to me, you will address me as drill sergeant, not sir, do you understand? I am a sergeant, not a sir. I work for a living."

So Bob said, "Yes, drill sergeant, I understand."

He then told Bob to stand up and drop his pants to see if he's a pussy or a man. Bob did as he was told. Poor guy had another hard-on. The drill sergeant couldn't believe his eyes.

He said: "My, my, my. Now that's what I call a man."

He looked at me and asked, "How much you got hanging, private?"

I told him, "It's about average, drill sergeant."

He then told Bob and myself to get off the bus and assemble into the columns. He continued to chew out each man, one for having long hair, one for saying "yes, sir," and so on until he reached the back of the bus. He walked back to the front of the bus and grabbed a guy sitting by the door and told him to get his sorry ass off his bus.

Then he said: "When I leave this bus, you all will have fifteen seconds to get your sorry asses off of my motherfucking bus to get in formation. The last one off will be pulling kitchen police duty for a week."

I never saw so many people get off a bus that fast. One poor guy had fallen down and everyone else was stepping and running over him. He had to be taken to the Base Hospital for medical care. After getting into a sorry-ass-looking formation, we heard a different sergeant lecture us in a memorized, highly prepared speech about what we were to expect from this night on. We were then marched to a nearby barracks. Again, a different sergeant picked out five of us for "fire watch" (to keep watch for any fires that may happen). We would be on watch for one hour each. Lucky me got picked first. I had been in the Army for less than twenty-four hours and I have already been assigned guard duty. Only the first of so many more to come.

That next morning at 5:00 am, this short E-5 "buck sergeant" (a newly promoted sergeant) came into the barracks yelling for everyone to get up and form up outside within five minutes. This buck sergeant was no more than five feet tall, but had a very commanding voice. He said we would march to the Mess Hall to eat in no more than ten minutes. He was sure right about the ten minutes, too. The last guy in our group had just sat down with his food when we were told to get in formation outside. He was pissed off, to say the least. Every morning for the next ten days, we would be awakened by this short sergeant at 5:00 am, get in formation, march to eat, come back for formation, and march off to other places.

The first day we were there, we marched to get our very short Army haircuts. As we were standing outside waiting for our turn to go into the barbershop, one guy who once had hair halfway down his back and a long beard, came out the doors crying. He no longer had a beard or any hair.

The black drill sergeant that was on the bus our first night came over to him and asked: "What the fuck is your problem, private. Do you miss your momma?"

The guy simply said, "They cut off all my hair."

That was the worst thing he could've said. The drill sergeant began cursing and calling him every name under the sun. He had the guy do push-ups until he could not pick any part of his body off the ground.

The drill sergeant said, "You would have made a fine Marine."

The next day, we marched over for dental and eye examinations. On the third day, we were given a lot of shots in both arms. The fourth day, we marched to this very large and old warehouse. We were told to take all of our clothing off and to put everything into the small box that was given to us and to send it all home or to throw it in the trash. It made no difference to the Army. The sergeant said we would have no use for any of it here at Fort Ord. One by one, we were given olive drab (OD) green underwear, OD green T-shirts, and OD green fatigue shirts and pants. Everything was OD green except our black boots. We also got a ball cap (or head cover). What do you think the color of it was? On the fifth day, we marched to another building and took a lot of tests. The questions were either true/false or multiple choice. When we were assembled in this large classroom, an NCO began telling us how the Army expected us to do our best on these lengthy tests in order for them to place us in the right Military Occupational Specialty (MOS). That first week of May 1968, I also received my first letter from Paula. She said she was doing fine and was getting bigger every day.

In Basic Infantry Training, we were doing lots of marching and drilling every day, M-14 Rifle Training, Physical Training (PT), Grenade Training, Gas Mask Training, Obstacle Course Training, Hand-to-Hand Combat Training, and Bayonet Training. Everywhere we marched, we had to carry that damn heavy M-14 rifle.

Bob was made acting corporal, a ranking just below sergeant. They told him he could have one acting private first class (PFC), a rank just below corporal, to help him with the other men. Guess who he picked? We now had the authority to tell the men what to do. One day during Hand-to-Hand Combat Training, Bob was paired up with this guy who was always giving him a hard time over his authority. The guy was a big man. He went to throw a punch at Bob, but as he did, Bob blocked it with his left hand and knocked him out with his right. He was knocked out cold with only one punch. The guy lay there lifeless for a good five minutes. After that, the guy never gave Bob a hard time.

One morning we marched to a classroom and Vietnam was the topic. We were told to pay attention because most of us would be going there. We watched a film about the people of Vietnam, how they made a living, and their living conditions. The film got into the war part. We watched men killing others and also being killed. As we sat there watching, no one moved or said a word. Everyone was tantalized by what we were seeing. After the film was over, the sergeant asked if we had any questions. We all respected this particular sergeant because we knew he had been to Vietnam and had even been wounded in a fire-fight (firing between two forces with small weapons) in his two tours of duty there. Everyone paid attention to every word as he spoke. I was hoping to never have to experience what he had gone through.

Basic Training, May 1968, at Fort Ord in California . . . right after they cut off all my hair!

After watching the film and asking questions for an hour and a half, we were given a short break. Mostly everyone went outside to have a smoke. As we were standing there, we noticed this private digging a hole in the sand with his hands. As the story goes, a drill sergeant saw this private throw his cigarette butt on the ground. In the Army, you are not to throw anything on the ground. After the hole was about a foot deep, the sergeant told the private to place the cigarette butt in the hole and then to fill the hole back up. After this was done, the sergeant asked the private if the cigarette butt had been put out.

Like a dumbass, the private said, "I don't know."

So the sergeant said to dig the butt back up to check.

The sergeant then said, "It looks to be out, so now you can rebury it."

Some of the men that had been smoking, including myself, quickly picked our cigarette butts off the ground. Our break was over by this time and we returned to the classroom.

For the next hour, the sergeant took and answered any questions we asked. Bob asked how long it took to make sergeant in the Army. The sergeant said he joined the Army in 1962, and after going through Basic Training and eight more weeks of Advanced Infantry Training (AIT), he was stationed in Germany for eighteen months and was only a PFC. He said he was told it was a lot easier to make rank in a war zone than in a non-war zone. In 1965 when the Vietnam

War was just beginning, he said he volunteered to go. After being in the country for only three weeks, he was promoted to specialist E-4 and after another eight months he was promoted to buck sergeant E-5. In 1967, he returned to Vietnam for another tour of duty. Just before he left, he was promoted to staff sergeant E-6. So to answer Bob's question, from private to staff sergeant took about four years and two tours to Vietnam. He said at the moment he was up for sergeant first class E-7.

Later on that day, Bob said he was thinking about putting in for Vietnam so he would be sure to get in after Basic Training.

He said, "If I'm going to make a career of the Army, then I would like to move up in rank as fast as possible, and Vietnam sounds like the place to do it."

I told him he was nuts. The next day he volunteered for Vietnam.

One day we were marching to Grenade Training Course and the drill sergeant giving the course showed us how to throw a live grenade for the first time. He showed us how to hold it in one hand and how to pull the pin and throw it at the target with the other hand. We could tell this one guy, by the name of Benson, was real nervous so we all paid closer attention to him as he went to pull the pin. He pulled the pin and dropped the grenade between the drill sergeant and me. After pulling the pin, you have about five to ten seconds before it explodes. The guy took off running. The drill sergeant reached down for the grenade and threw it. He then took off after the guy, calling him every name under the sun.

On the next to last week of Basic Training, we were marched ten miles out to an obstacle course for low crawling under live fire. By the time we arrived there, the sun was just setting. The obstacle course was fifty yards long and thirty yards wide. Ten men at a time would low crawl on their stomachs while M-60 machine guns were firing live ammunition over their heads. Spaced at intervals were live explosives that would explode at any given time. A mound of earth piled around each one. We were told to stay away from the mounds as best we could. To make matters even worse and more intense, there was barbed wire about two feet above the entire length of the obstacle course. When the machine guns began firing, the first ten men would start crawling under the wire. I was in the first group of men. We crawled through loose dirt and sand. The sand was very hard to crawl through and you would get tired quickly, even a nineteen-year-old. I told myself I would be the first one to get through the course. I started crawling as fast as I could but the dirt and sand was getting in my eyes, so I had a hard time seeing where I was going. I had gone about twenty feet when the first explosive went off, throwing dirt, sand, and small pebbles of stone into the air and back down on top of us. I was getting sweat in my eyes along with the dirt and sand. It made it even harder to see anything. The next thing I knew, I was right beside this mound of dirt. I was thinking, "Oh shit." As I got a few feet away from it, the thing exploded. My head hurt, my ears were ringing, and for a minute I didn't know where I was. When I came to my senses, I returned to crawling. I finally made my way to the end of the course. I was next to last to finish of the ten men. At least I was not the last one. As we stood there watching the other men on the obstacle course, I was wondering if this was what it was going to be like in Vietnam.

About this time, I saw Bob crawling alongside Benson, the kid who had dropped the live grenade. Bob was trying to pull him away from one of the mounds of dirt with the explosive. Benson was so scared that he crawled on top of one of the mounds. The sergeants were going crazy trying to get his attention, but he could not hear them because there was so much noise from the M-60s and explosives going off. Then, the mound that Benson was laying on went off and threw him up into the barbed wire and then back down. We all knew he was dead. By the time the sergeants got the firing and explosives to stop, they got him into a medivac chopper twenty minutes later. He was in very bad shape, but still alive as the chopper took him away. Bob was sitting on the ground crying, so I went over to him. He kept saying he should've done more over and over again. I'll never forget that night or the next morning.

At formation the next morning, our flag was at half-staff with an M-14 rifle with a bayonet that fits on the end sticking in the ground with a helmet sitting on top of it. Beside the rifle to its right, there was a pair of Army boots that were "spit-shined" polished. The company's first sergeant called everyone to attention. He said at 2:14 am on the night of June 17, 1968, Private Gary Benson passed away from wounds he received in the line of duty for his country. Following that, "Taps" played. I looked around and there were many wet eyes, mine included. Private Benson was a stupid fuck-up, but he was our stupid fuck-up. He should not have been allowed to enter the Army. Everyone was sad for his loss. It was my first experience with death in the military. It would not be my last either. For the rest of the day we had no training or duty.

A few days before the end of June, we made our last formation.

During that last formation, the black drill sergeant that called all of us a bunch of pussies and queers that night on the bus said: "I do not see one pussy or queer today. All I see are the best damn men in the Army."

This statement brought the predictable cheers from us troops.

He said, "As I call out your name, come forward to receive orders for your next duty stations, and then you are free to leave."

As our names were called out in alphabetical order, Bob went just before me since his last name was Long and mine is Lott. We received a big yellow manila envelope with our orders inside. Bob's orders had him staying at Fort Ord for eight more weeks of AIT. He was to report for AIT the next day on the other side of the base. After AIT, he would be going to Vietnam after some leave time. My orders had me going to Germany by way of Fort Dix, New Jersey, for three days. I was to be assigned to a transportation company as a heavy truck driver without going through AIT. Typically, everyone goes through AIT after Basic Training, but I got on-the-job training (OJT) instead. I received ten days' leave before reporting to Fort Dix. I went to the pay phone and called Paula. I told her I would be flying into Tulsa some time tomorrow. Bob and I went off to find a cold beer. After a few cold ones, I had to go and catch my ride home. I told Bob that after I got to Germany I would write and send him my address. We had the last beer for Private Benson, may he rest in peace.

It was the last day of June when I arrived at the Tulsa International Airport. I glanced at my wristwatch and saw it was just past 8:00 pm. I went to the front of the terminal building with my Army duffel bag and got a cab. I paid the driver $10 for the twenty-five miles or so it took to get to Hominy. The cabbie asked me where I had been stationed and I told him I had just finished Basic Training at Fort Ord, California. The cabbie drove on in silence. Once inside my small hometown, I directed his turns from the highway to where we lived. I was so tired and so happy at the same time to be home. The 1955 Chevy sure looked good sitting in the driveway.

The cabbie said, "Good luck in Germany," and drove away.

I could see from the driveway that the lights were still on in the living room along with the television. I was so excited and happy to be home. I stepped onto the front porch and knocked on the door. Paula answered the door and we hugged and kissed. We sat and talked for a while. I was so happy, but at the same time, so tired from the trip and from getting up every morning at 5:00 am. Paula was getting really big. I asked her how the baby was and she said she could have it at any time. She was right. On July 2, 1968, I had to rush her to the hospital after only two days back home. She gave birth to a boy, Paul A. Lott. As of this writing, my son just turned forty-eight years old.

With the few days at home gone, it was time to leave for Fort Dix, New Jersey. After saying our goodbyes with lots of hugs and kisses at the Tulsa International Airport, Paula drove the old-but-still-running '55 Chevy back home. We promised to write each other as soon as I could send her my new address. As for me, I was on my way to Germany.

CHAPTER 5

Fort Dix, New Jersey

I arrived at Fort Dix around the middle of July. I reported in around noon. The specialist E-4 company clerk took my orders for Germany and said I would be leaving in about three days. Until then, I would be staying in a holding company and put on some kind of duty like Kitchen Police (KP) or guard duty. He then gave me the directions to the barracks I would be staying in for the next three days. The barracks were an old wooden building. It looked like it could fall over at any time. I went inside to an empty barracks. I walked to the far end so I could have a cot next to the wall. As I began to make my bed, I noticed on the floor, beneath the cot and next to the wall, an Army fatigue shirt that had sergeant E-5 stripes on it. The nametag on it said "King." It seemed to be about my size, so I tried it on and it fit just right. About this time, other men came into the barracks.

They came up to me and one private said, "Sergeant King, are these other cots taken or not?"

I said, "I am not a . . ." and then stopped myself.

I continued and said, "Take any cot you like."

I thought to myself, *I could have some fun with these sergeant stripes. Or I could get into a lot of trouble for impersonating a sergeant.*

As I was locking my duffel bag to my Army cot to keep it safe, this sergeant first class E-7 came walking over to me. He looked at my nametag and said: "Sergeant King, I am in charge of this holding company. As you are the only sergeant here, I am putting you in charge of the fire watch detail tonight. You will pick nine men to stand watch for one hour each starting at 9:00 pm until 6:00 am. Do you understand?"

I said, "Yes, sergeant."

He then said: "You seem a little nervous. How long have you been a sergeant?"

I answered, "Not very long."

Before he left, he said, "If we get other sergeants, you will not have fire watch detail tomorrow night."

I started thinking to myself that this sergeant thing may have been a big mistake. I was getting an urgent need for food, so I left to find a Mess Hall and eat some chow. I found one, then walked back to the barracks, pissed off at having fire watch detail on my first night here. This PFC with one stripe had just thrown a cigarette butt on the ground.

I said, "Hey, dumbass, don't you know better than to throw a cigarette butt on the ground?"

He answered, "Yes, sir."

I said: "Sir? Did you just call me a sir? I am not a sir, I am a sergeant. I work for a living. You will address me as sergeant, is that understood?"

He answered, "Yes, sergeant."

I said to him, "Pick up that butt and put it in the can behind you."

As I turned around to leave, I saw a captain (a commissioned officer) standing there. I came to attention and gave him a salute. I was thinking he was going to chew me out for the way I had spoken to the PFC.

He said, "Sergeant King, how long have you been a sergeant?"

I said, "Sir, I just received my stripes today."

He told me that he had been watching me with the PFC, and that I had been doing a fine job with him. Then he turned and left.

By the time I got back to the barracks, it was full. There were about thirty or so men there, plus three E-5 sergeants, so I would not be doing fire detail the next night. I had to pick nine men for fire watch, so I had all of the privates, PFCs, and specialist E-4s write their names on a piece of paper and put it in a can. I told them that the nine names I pulled out would be on fire watch tonight in the order they were picked. There were nine very unhappy soldiers. But what was I to do? I was the sergeant in charge. The next morning after chow, I went looking for a pay phone to call Paula. She said everything was fine. I told her that after I had gotten to Germany I would see what I had to do to bring her over.

The next day we had formation. Two trucks were parked nearby. They were two-and-a-half-ton trucks, the exact kind I would be driving in Germany.

The sergeant E-7 said, "When your name is called, get your gear and get on those trucks as you will be taken to the airport and be on your way to your new duty station."

Most everyone's name was called but mine. None of these men were going to Germany. They were all on their way to Vietnam. I was thinking now is the time to take off this shirt before I get caught wearing it. In about an hour, another formation was called and I would be leaving for Germany as soon as I went and got my gear. As I was about to leave, I threw the shirt back beneath the cot and next to the wall where I had found it. Maybe some other private would find it and have as much fun as I did, or maybe they would be a little smarter than I was and leave it be. Sergeant King, wherever you are, I would like to say thank you for the shirt. I had fun being you.

CHAPTER 6

Germany

We boarded a huge plane specifically chartered for hauling GIs. It was the same plane used on commercial flights, and it even carried attractive young stewardesses. In no time, we took off going east out over the Atlantic Ocean. I had never seen so much water before. I would be seeing a lot more in the eight hours it took to fly to Germany. The flight attendants aboard the DC-8 Jet Mainliner were immediately busy with the passengers. There were 250 of us and a crew of eight, including those in the cockpit and the flight attendants. There were two in-flight movies that were shown on several pull-down screens and plenty of food, snacks, and beverages. No beer or alcohol of any kind was being served. Our pilot made the announcement that we would be in the air for the next eight hours, and that the trip to Germany was 3,845 miles, give or take. He assured us that they would try to make our trip as comfortable as possible.

After looking out at the ocean for two hours, I had seen all the water I cared to see. I tried to sleep to pass the time, but with no luck. Some people can close their eyes and go right to sleep. Not me. I have to be very tired in order to fall asleep. I closed my eyes and tried to think of Paula and our new baby. I tried to think of Bob and the times we had at Fort Ord. I tried to think of my brother Carl in Vietnam, what he was doing—was he out of the jungle, was he safe—and so on. I had to take a piss, so I got up and walked to the back of the plane.

While I was waiting my turn for the bathroom, or should I say the latrine, the same private I told to pick up the cigarette butt came out of the latrine and looked at me and said: "Don't I know you? You were a sergeant at Fort Dix."

I said, "I was at Fort Dix, but I'm a private just like you."

He left, but every time he saw me after that he would take a long look at me.

After eight hours in the air, the pilot came on the PA and told us we would be landing in twenty minutes. We landed at Rhein-Main Airport in Frankfurt. After getting off the plane and finding our duffel bags, we were loaded into the deuce-and-a-half-ton trucks waiting for us. We were then taken by convoy to the Frankfurt Train Station. From there it was a two-hour train ride to the town of

Stuttgart. It was my first train ride. After arriving in Stuttgart, our paperwork was checked to see who was going where. Three other guys and I were going to the 396 Transportation Company just outside of a small town by the name of Boblingen. The rest of the men were going to other places, and some were staying right there in Stuttgart.

By now, it was just past midnight when a specialist E-4 came over to the four of us and checked our papers. He said he would be taking us to our company. He was driving an OD green vehicle. It was a four-door 1966 Chevrolet Biscayne. It would be my first ride in an official Army car, but certainly not my last. I was the first one of us four to reach the car so I got in the front seat, riding shotgun. The other three had to ride in the back. The specialist E-4 said it was a twenty-five-minute ride to our company. We pulled in the front gate and were stopped by two military police (MPs). After checking our orders, they let us go on our way. The driver drove to the far backside of the base. We pulled up in front of this three-story, very old rock building that seemed to be about fifty yards long. Out front was a large sign that said "Home of the 396 Transportation Company." In other words, my home for the next year. The driver let us out, said goodbye, and left. The four of us went inside and reported to the sergeant on duty. He showed us to some Army cots and said we could sleep in tomorrow, as it was 2:30 am. He said tomorrow after we got up to report back to the Orderly Room (OR) and we would be assigned a room with other men.

After being assigned to my new living quarters, I made my cot and put away my gear. There were fifteen other cots in the room. I was the only one there except for one guy who was already asleep. I was told that he had guard duty the previous night and that he'd be off duty today. I was getting hungry so I went to find the Mess Hall, but it was closed until 5:30 that evening. I went back to the OR and asked if I could leave the barracks to find some place to eat. The first sergeant E-8 told me I was free to go, but to be back in time to make morning formation at 6:00 am. He then informed me that I did not have to ask permission to leave the barracks if I was off duty. As I was leaving the barracks, I ran into the other three guys. We all had the same idea. We all had been given different rooms because one was a cook, one a clerk, and the other was a truck driver, like me. We found a pizza place, ate, and then went looking for the Post Exchange (PX). After getting what we needed, we went looking for the base movie theater and bowling alley, for future reference. We went back to the barracks, and I was still the only one there except for the guy sleeping.

With nothing to do, I wrote Bob and my brother Carl a letter and gave them my address. About this time, some of the men came in and introduced themselves. I went back to writing a few lines to Paula and my new address. All the men in my room were either a PFC or a specialist E-4. I was the only private E-2, the low man on the totem pole. I left to find the mailroom then returned and hit the hay. The next morning at 6:00 am, we made company formation in the back of our building. We went to morning chow afterward and then back to our rooms to make our beds and clean up the barracks. We were then off to the motor pool about a block away. My squad leader came over and introduced himself as Sergeant E-5 Dixon.

He took me over to this deuce-and-a-half truck and said: "This will be your truck. You will be responsible for it. Check and see if it needs fuel. If so, drive it over and fill it up."

I told him, "Okay, but I have never driven one before."

He replied, "Did you not go through AIT?"

I said, "No, I was OJT."

The sergeant then gave me a two-hour class on driving. At AIT, it would have been eight weeks.

In Germany, we worked five days a week with Saturday and Sunday off unless we had to pull KP or guard duty. My first guard duty sucked because it was on a Friday night. When you pull guard duty, you have the next day off. Seeing that the next day was already Saturday, I got screwed. I reported to the Guard Building that evening with four other guys. We were put on a three-quarter-ton truck and drove to the first stop. On the next stop, I was assigned duty guarding a very old building in the very back of our base. It looked as if it could have fallen down at any time. The driver let me out and I asked if we had any ammunition for our rifles.

He said, "No, only the MPs carry ammunition."

After he left, I thought to myself, *At least we could have one bullet to carry in our shirt pocket like Barney on the "Andy Griffith Show."*

Towards the end of that July, everything was going good for me—except I hadn't received any mail from anyone.

CHAPTER 7

August 1968

That August was very hot in Germany. The nights were a little cool. It was perfect weather during guard duty usually. I typically had to pull guard duty about once a week. The second week in August, I got to go off base and ride shotgun with this black guy. His name was Foster, a specialist E-4 pay grade from somewhere in the state of New Jersey. I was to go with him for the month of August to get to know my way around Germany and to find out how to get to the other military bases. Foster was a cool guy and we became good friends. We drove off the base and after a few miles got onto the German Autobahn. That meant there was no speed limit. The cars were humming along, passing us like we were sitting still. Our truck had a governor on it, an automatic speed-control device, so our top speed was only fifty-five miles per hour. Our first stop was twenty miles away. After getting the truck loaded, we took off for our next stop, about twenty-five more miles on down the Autobahn. By this time, it was late afternoon. We arrived at the next base and after getting the cargo unloaded, we were off to find the Mess Hall and a place to stay for the night because we were not allowed to drive on the Autobahn at night.

The next day we headed back to our base because we had no more pickups or deliveries. On the way back, a red convertible with four girls inside, possibly in their early twenties, passed us while honking their car horn and waving their hands. We watched as they turned off at the next exit. About thirty minutes later, the same car with the same four girls passed us again. This time, they got in front of us and slowed down to around our speed. The two girls in the back seat began to wave and blow us kisses. By this time, Foster and I were waving back and blowing them kisses, too. What happened next, however, made our day. The two girls in the back seat pulled off their tops and bras. These were the biggest breasts I had ever seen. They gave us one nice show, let me tell you. The girls gave us a big kiss and wave and then they sped away. That was the last time we ever saw them. We arrived back at our company around noon, and after parking the truck at the motor pool, our squad leader, Sergeant Dixon, came over to me and asked how my first trip went and if I saw anything interesting.

I said, "It was a good trip, and I did see a few things that got my attention and got my interest 'up.'"

For the rest of August, I rode shotgun with Foster and we had a good time getting to know each other. Foster had been in Germany for two years, with one more to go. He was thinking about staying in the Army because where he came from, there were not any good-paying jobs. He said his family was poor and having a hard time getting by. He was sending them half of his money each month when we got paid. The last week of August we stayed on base and I had guard duty, not fun because it had been raining all day. I was hoping it would stop by the time I went on duty, but no luck. It rained all night. At least I had the next day off and could sleep in.

After getting up and around, I walked over to the PX to get a few things I had run out of. I went to a movie theater at the base by myself just to be alone. I was getting homesick and missing Paula. Halfway through the movie, I got up and went back to the barracks and wrote Paula a nice long letter.

CHAPTER 8

September 1968

It's the second week of September and Army life is pretty good except when you have KP or guard duty on the weekends. Every day you get up and make morning formation at 5:00 am so the first sergeant can call your name and see that you are still present or Absent Without Leave (AWOL). We then would clean our rooms, go to chow, and then off to the motor pool just to sit around and wait for midday chow. Then we would go back to the motor pool and wait for evening chow. Some days, we did work, such as washing our trucks and pulling maintenance on them. Army life in Germany was a lot different from Army life in Basic Training. The sergeants didn't mess with you, unless you were a fuck-up or a fuck-off. You do as you are told and life is good. I was hoping to drive my truck off base by myself for the first time since I knew where most of the other bases were.

After getting off work one day, I went to the mailroom and had gotten three letters—one from Paula, one from Bob, and the last from Carl. Paula said that everything back home was fine and that the baby was doing good and that she missed and loved me. The letter from Bob said that he had just finished AIT and that he was home on leave for ten days before going to Vietnam. He said on the last day of AIT he was given a promotion to private first class (PFC) E-3 pay grade, mainly for trying to help Private Benson in Basic Training. He said after he got to his new company in Vietnam, he would send his new address.

In Carl's letter, he said he was glad that I got the duty station in Germany. He said he didn't know how the rest of Vietnam was, but where he was, it was pure hell. He said they came into base camp where all the REMFs were after being out for ten days thumping through the hot jungle while carrying heavy loads on their backs and walking through leech-infested waters. He said three weeks earlier, they went out with thirty men and came back with twenty-two. They had three that were KIA and five that were WIA. He said they were crossing this stream when all hell broke loose. He and two other guys had just gotten to the other side and were helping the other men out of the water when the VC opened up on them. They had set up an ambush on them. When all was said and done, ten of them were dead. The choppers came in and the dead and wounded were taken away. The rest of them got on choppers and were returned to their base camp for a few days of rest before going back out.

    After reading Carl's letter, I was very thankful I was stationed in Germany. One Saturday I went off base with Foster, a new guy. The town of Boblingen was just a half-mile away, so with nothing to do, we went sightseeing. The town was very clean. We saw people sweeping the street in front of their shops. We found a bar and went inside for a beer. Just down the street was a movie theater so we went inside. After thirty minutes of hearing nothing but German, we got up and went to find another beer and something to eat. The town of Boblingen was a nice little place and the German people were very friendly to us. After returning to our barracks, several of us got a poker game going. For the next three hours, we drank beer while listening to rock 'n' roll music. I came away winning a total of $2.75.

CHAPTER 9

October 1968

In October, I finally got my first assignment to take a truck off base by myself. Until then, I had been riding shotgun with Foster. I left early one morning, and it felt good driving my truck off base alone. My destination was an Army depot not far from Stuttgart. Foster and I had gone to a lot of bases, but this one was a first for me. With no trouble at all, I arrived at the depot, a large warehouse filled with rows of new truck tires. With my truck loaded up with tires, I headed back. The trip there and back took up most of the morning. I would go back to the same place a few more times in the coming months. Going off base with Foster was nice, but going off by myself was so much better. At times, it almost felt like I wasn't in the Army. I was just my own boss. I enjoyed driving the truck, though I didn't like the large steering wheel. I was never able to get used to it. For the month of October, I went off base driving to three or four other bases. By the end of October, the mornings were beginning to get a little cool.

CHAPTER
10

November 1968

November was when the cold hit. The daytime temperature was in the forties and the thirties at night. No letters this month from Paula or Carl, but I had one from Bob, his first since he got to Vietnam. He said he was in this place called Chu Lai, up north near the A Shau Valley. He was an infantryman in the Americal Division. He said on his first night, they were hit by rockets that killed two of their medics. They were out on a search-and-destroy mission in the Chu Lai area, just moving through the bush and sweeping the area. The enemy artillery came up from behind them. They had eight WIA and two KIA. He said they were currently back at Chu Lai, but were going back out soon. He said he was beginning to think that he may have done the wrong thing by volunteering for Vietnam. His only wish was for me to write him back a few lines about the German girls.

Near the end of November, we had a big fight in the room across the hall from ours. One end of the room was some guys playing country music, the other end was playing rock 'n' roll, and the middle of the room was playing soul music. The guys playing country turned up the volume, so in return the rock 'n' roll guys turned up their volume. The soul music guys retaliated by turning theirs up, too. The music kept getting louder until everyone was calling each other names. Things were flying all over the room. Two guys had gotten so drunk they could not walk without falling down. The MPs had to come in and take the two drunks out.

I had guard duty and KP the last week of November. My guard duty was inside of this building with very big rooms. It looked to be some kind of place for officers. There was about a dozen large rooms with very dim lighting. The place resembled one of those horror movies where at any time, someone would jump out in front of you with a big sharp knife. Every so often, I would hear a crackling or a popping sound. My duty was to walk around inside the place. Why? I don't know. I guess it was to keep the ghosts company. It was almost midnight when my replacement arrived. I was sure glad because I had all the goosebumps and excitement I could handle for one night. On the way back to the barracks, the driver asked if I had seen any ghosts in the building. He said he had heard stories about the place being occupied by ghosts.

CHAPTER
11

December 1968

The first week of December we got a foot of snow. I remember those bitter cold German mornings when we would make morning formation outside at 6:00 am. The morning formation on December 19th, snow was coming down and a cold wind was blowing in our faces, and the first sergeant said that when he called our names we had to come forward. My name and two other names were called. I was trying to remember if I had done anything wrong. The two other guys were promoted to specialist E-4, the same grade as a corporal. I was promoted to PFC with one stripe on my sleeve. I was glad to get the promotion and to finally be getting more money, but at the same time I was too cold to care. I was thinking, *you could have given these to us in the warm building, you dumbass first sergeant.* That evening, Foster and a few of the guys took me to the Enlisted Men's (EM) Club for a beer to celebrate my promotion to PFC.

December 1968 as a PFC in Germany

CHAPTER 12

January 1969

At one point in January, we had three feet of snow covering the ground and everything else in sight. All of the trucks were grounded from leaving the base until the roads became better. One Saturday, I recall not having KP or guard duty, so a few of us went to the base movie theater to see "Butch Cassidy and the Sundance Kid," featuring Paul Newman and Robert Redford. The movie was pretty damn good, but walking in all that snow was a bad idea. I fell head first into the snow on the way back, and everyone seemed to think it was funny except for me.

Beer is not allowed in the barracks, and sometimes we would have surprise inspections. About 8:00 that night, a friend of ours who was on guard duty in the Orderly Room came running into our room saying that the first sergeant and the commanding officer (CO) were pulling a surprise inspection in the next thirty minutes. Everyone was either drinking beer, smoking weed, or both. The scene of everyone running around trying to get rid of all the empty beer cans was hysterical. The unopened cans were thrown out of the two-story building into the snow below. Air fresheners were sprayed throughout the building. The first sergeant and CO, a new lieutenant just out of Officer Candidate School (OCS), came into our room, walked around, and then left without saying a word. The first sergeant had a funny expression on his face as he followed the CO out the door.

About thirty minutes later the sergeant returned and said: "You all had better go get those beer cans out of the snow before they freeze. And bring me one."

After drinking the beer he said, "You all know that beer is not allowed in the barracks, and stop smoking that damn weed in my barracks."

Then he left.

The first sergeant had been in the Army for almost thirty years and was about to retire in September. He was a cool first sergeant, maybe because he was one of us many years ago and knew what it was like to be alone so far from home. Mostly everyone had the highest respect for him. As long as you did your job to the best of your ability and stayed out of major trouble, he would stand up for you. For the rest of my time in the Army, I never would meet a better first sergeant.

CHAPTER 13

February 1969

You guessed it, it was still cold here. The sun had not been out in a long damn time. I'm not a cold weather person. I like it best in the summer. The snow stays on the ground most of all the winter in Germany. Back in Oklahoma, it would snow one foot one day and be gone the next, but not here. Oh well, life goes on. I had guard duty and KP in the same week. KP duty sucks big time. On KP duty, you get up two hours before everyone else and help get food ready. After chow, you have to clean the dining room, sweep and mop the floors, and clean the tables of the food left on them where some asshole missed his mouth. After that, you have to wash all of the plates, cups, glassware, silverware, and pots and pans. The most famous job of them all, however, is peeling all the potatoes. We have them at every meal, so that will tell you how many there always are to peel. After all that is done, you get ready for the noon meal and evening meal. You have to stay until everything gets done. Usually, there were four or five of us on KP at a time. With 150 in our company, KP was no fun.

I had a funny letter waiting for me from Carl when I got off KP duty. I typically get one from him about once a month, but this time it was almost two months. He said every time they are out in the bush, planes would fly over and spray a heavy red-colored substance everywhere. Their fatigues would be covered with the red spray. They would try to cover their noses and mouths to keep them from coughing and choking. Someone said it was called "Agent Orange." It was a defoliant sprayed by the military for the purpose of killing everything that was green that offered concealment to the enemy. They were told that the chemical was not harmful to people. A week later, they went back to that same location and everything green was now dead. He told me that he got promoted to buck sergeant E-5 with three stripes. He also told me that he was glad to hear about my promotion. He informed me that with his new promotion, he's also Walking Point. He said it felt good to be out in front. He said a lot of the Walking-Points make a lot of noise because they're from the city and don't know how to walk without making any noise. He said he got tired of it, so one day he asked for the job. Carl said that he's the oldest man in his unit at just twenty-four, except for the first sergeant, who has been in the Army for seventeen years. Everyone calls him "Pops," but not to his face.

He said one night around midnight, they were in the bush and he felt a shit coming so he left the perimeter. He reminded me that you always had to leave the perimeter out of regard for your buddies. He said it was so dark you could hardly see your hand right in front of your face. He barely made it in time. He said he walked out a ways, let it fly, finished up, and crept back to his place and sacked out.

The next morning he heard one very pissed-off soldier yelling: "Who was the asshole that shit all over my boots? If I ever find out, you will be one sorry ass."

Everyone tried to blame this new guy they had gotten a few days earlier.

Carl then asked how I liked driving my truck all over Germany. It made me feel a little guilty about it, being in a safe place while he was walking through the jungle not knowing if or when he was going to be shot at. I told Carl that when we both got back home we would have one big party.

The last week in February, I pulled Charge of Quarters (CQ) duty. That's when you report to the Orderly Room from 6:00 pm until 6:00 am the next morning. Your duty is to answer any phone calls. If it's an emergency requiring prompt action, then you have to wake up the first sergeant. It better be an emergency if you ever have to do that, though. Thank God I never had an emergency like that. One other duty you had during CQ was at 5:00 am, when you had to go around to all the rooms and wake everyone up for the day. Then it would be your turn to climb into bed. I only had to pull CQ duty a few times.

CHAPTER 14

March 1969

I woke up on March 2, 1969, and it was my twentieth birthday. The snow was still on the ground and it was cold in the barracks. The heat had gone off some time during the night. Some of us went to the EM Club that night to celebrate my birthday.

The following day, I was gone the entire time picking up truck parts and taking them to other bases. That week, I had been to seven other bases. Near the end of March, I pulled guard duty yet again. When I reported for guard duty, the sergeant of the guard had four of us line up. He told the first guy to bring his rifle to port arms (a movement to bring the rifle pointing upward to the left). The guy forgot how it was done. The next guy did it all wrong, too. The third guy almost dropped his rifle. At this point, I could tell he was getting pissed off.

He then came to me and said, "PFC Lott, do you know how to bring your weapon to port arms?"

I answered, "Yes, sergeant."

He then said, "Come to port arms."

So I did. Since I was the only one who knew what to do, I was dismissed from guard duty and got to enjoy the night off.

As I was walking away, I could hear the sergeant calling out to the three other solders, "Bring your weapon to port arms!"

CHAPTER
15

April 1969

One day in the middle of April, I went by the mailroom when I got off work at the motor pool and found there was still no mail from Bob or Paula. I did, however, get a letter from my brother Charles, Carl's twin brother. He told me he had some bad news about Carl. Sometime in February while being Walking Point in the A Shau Valley, Carl's company got ambushed by a company of VC. There were VC snipers in the trees. He said they opened up with machine guns, mortars, and RPGs (rocket-propelled grenades). Almost everyone in his unit was either killed or wounded. Carl was shot in his left leg and left hip. He was medivacked out to Japan for three weeks and then to Fort Lewis, Washington. Charles said Carl would be there until he got out of the Army in October. He said that he talked to him via telephone, and that he would be all right. He said he would be in the Base Hospital for quite some time. He said he had only two more months to go in Vietnam when he got shot. For most of the preceding ten months, he had been in the bush. Carl relayed a message to me saying not to worry about him and that we will have that party when I come home. This is the kind of news you don't care to get. I was just grateful that he was still alive. I wrote him a letter telling him so and letting him know how much he meant to me and how much I loved him. Speaking of love, I've been getting less mail from Paula these days. I was getting one or two letters a week, but now it's maybe one every other week. I also haven't received any letters from Bob lately. It left me worrying about him.

It finally started to warm up in Germany. I didn't have KP or guard duty for a few weeks. One Friday, a few of us had plans to go downtown to check out the bars in Boblingen. When it came time to leave and get our passes to get off base, we found out everyone was grounded, and our trip was canceled. We never did find out why that happened. Instead, we had a few beers and played some poker. I came out on top with $1.25. It wasn't much, but it was sure better than losing $1.25.

We had another fight in the barracks. It was a verbal disagreement at first, and then it turned into a knock-down after knock-down by one guy and then the other. The MPs had to be called. They took away the two guys, and it was a month before they got to return. The two had been put in the stockade for thirty days. We never did find out what the fight was about.

CHAPTER 16

May 1969

No mail still from Paula and Bob. It's been three weeks now and nothing from either of them. I got another letter from Carl, though. He said he was doing a lot better. He said he could walk some with the use of a cane. He said he would be in the hospital for another two weeks, and then he would have a medical profile—with no running, jumping, or standing for over five minutes at a time—for the remainder of his time in the Army. He reminded me that he was glad I was in Germany and not Vietnam. I was thinking the exact same thing.

By now, I knew my way around Germany pretty well. For the last two weeks I have been taking this new guy with me, the same way that I had gone with Foster when I first got there. The guy was all right except that he talked too much. One Saturday night, three of us guys got a pass to go downtown to a bar we had been hearing a lot about. It was a bar for young people our age. We got a table and ordered some German beer. It wasn't good. Three girls approached us and asked if we would like some company. How could we turn them down? They were American but living there while attending school. They were all from well-to-do families—very rich. We sat and talked and got to know one another. We had to be back on base before midnight or we could get written up for being AWOL. The girls all lived together in an apartment and asked if we would like to take them there for a drink. It was very tempting, but we only had a half-hour to get back on base. As we got up to leave, Pam, the one I had been talking to, gave me her phone number and said to give her a call sometime. After getting a taxi, we arrived back at the front gate with five minutes to spare. The MP at the gate took a look at his watch and waved us through. I never gave Pam too much thought after that night because I was married and I took it very seriously.

I went to the mailroom the next day after getting off work, and still no mail from Bob or Paula. I was getting this feeling that something may have happened to Bob. I also could not understand why Paula had not been writing. I wrote to her mother and asked if everything was all right with Paula, but she never wrote back either.

CHAPTER 17

June 1969

The first week of June came and went, and still no mail from Bob or Paula. I was really beginning to worry about him. I had no duty one day after guard duty so I went over to the personnel building where a friend of mine worked. Pete was a PFC, like myself. He was a good friend and also one of the guys who went to town that night when I got Pam's phone number. I gave Bob's name and mailing address to Pete and asked if I could find out if he was okay because it had been so long since I'd heard from him. Pete said he would see what he could do, but that it may take a while. A week went by and still there was no word from Pete about Bob, but I did finally get a letter from Paula.

She said: "I'll come right to the point of this letter. I have been seeing someone else, and I am asking you for a divorce. Our marriage is not working out. I wasn't ready when we got married, and the only reason I agreed was because I was pregnant."

That's about all the letter said. My head was spinning. I could not believe what I had just read. I sat there and read it over and over again. On top of that, I had CQ duty. Just before going on CQ duty, Pete came walking up to me not looking too good.

He said, "I have some bad news about your friend in Vietnam."

I asked, "Is he dead?"

Pete said, "Yes."

He handed me a piece of paper that basically said, "On the fourteenth of December 1968, Specialist Bob Long was killed in action while on patrol."

It went on to say that his unit had walked into an ambush and Bob had been killed by an RPG. Bob was only in Vietnam for three months. I could not believe it. First the letter from Paula, now this. What in the world was happening? Pete said not to tell anyone or he could get in a lot of trouble for doing what he did for me. I promised him I would not tell anyone how I found out.

I reported to CQ duty and couldn't stop thinking about the letter from Paula and about the news of Bob. It's hard putting my feelings to words. I was sad, heartbroken, mad, and pissed-off all at the same time. To top it all off, there was not a thing I could do about either one. I was sitting by the phone feeling sorry for myself. I had to talk to someone. I reached into my pocket and pulled out Pam's phone number. I dialed it.

She answered and said, "This is Pam."

I said: "Hello, this is Paul. Do you remember me? You gave me your number two weeks ago."

She said, "Yes, I was hoping to see you again."

We talked for one straight hour. She asked when I was coming back to the club, and I told her I had no duty the coming weekend and could be there then. I told her I would give her a call as soon as I found out for sure. I don't know why I called her. It may have been because I was feeling sad and lonesome for lack of company. For the next week, I was feeling pretty low. I had put in for a pass for the weekend since I had no duty of any kind.

For the next week, the days seemed to stand still and the nights were even worse. Time seemed to go by very slowly. I could not stop thinking about the letter from Paula. I thought about Private Benson in Basic Training, about my brother Carl being shot, and about Bob being killed in Vietnam. When Friday rolled around, I called Pam to tell her that I had a pass for the weekend.

She said, "What if I were to pick you up at the front gate around 6:00 pm on Friday?"

She told me to look for a red car. When I arrived at the front gate, I showed my pass to the MP on duty, and he asked if the girl in the red convertible was waiting on me. I told him she was.

He said: "You lucky dog. Ask her if she has a girlfriend for me."

After getting into the car and saying our hellos, she asked if I was hungry. We drove to this little café that was out of the way. We sat and ate and talked for what seemed to be a very long time.

I asked her, "How come you picked me when you could have the pick of someone else?"

She said: "Most guys are juvenile-acting or jerks. The moment I saw and talked to you, I could tell you were different. You seemed happy-go-lucky."

She told me that her family was from New York, and that her father was American and her mother German. She said she came to Germany to go to school and learn about the German people. Her father made a fortune in real estate by buying property, houses and land. Pam was twenty-two years old, about 5'5", with long blond hair and blue eyes. In other words, she was very pretty. We sat and talked about everything, from her family to me being the youngest of ten kids.

I then asked her, "How come you have not asked about my wedding ring?"

She said: "I'm young. I don't care if you are married or not, but I prefer married men because there is no commitment. Plus, I don't plan to ever get married."

Then she asked, "Do you love your wife?"

I said, "Yes."

But then I had to tell her about the letter I had received from Paula. She told me she was sorry for me. Then I told her about the news about Bob being killed in Vietnam. I told her that up until then, everything had been going just fine. I told her that because of all that, I ended up calling her because I had to get away and talk to someone.

She said: "Let's go and have some fun. I promise to make you feel better."

She would not let me pay for the meal or anything else that night. We drove to an old building in Stuttgart. She said it's where all the young people went to drink and dance. I'm not a dancer, but after a few beers Pam got me on that dance floor. Around 9:00 pm we left and went to her apartment. It was in the rich part of town. There was a doorman, and the only way you could get in was if he knew who you were. As he opened the door for us, Pam handed him $20. It was a very big and nice apartment.

After a few drinks, I told her: "It's getting late. Maybe I should be getting back to the base."

Then she said, "You have a weekend pass, and I promised you that I would make you feel better."

She then suggested that we go for a swim. I told her I didn't have a swimming suit.

She replied: "Neither do I. We swim nude."

I was thinking, *This is too good to be true.*

We went to the pool, and Pam's two roommates were already there. Pam got undressed and jumped in. Here I am, standing there watching three nude girls swimming.

Pam asked, "Are you coming in?"

Well, what else could I do? I got out of my clothes and jumped in. After swimming for a while, we went back to her apartment. She fixed us a drink and put on some music.

She asked, "How's your day going so far?"

I said, "It couldn't get any better."

She said, "Yes, it can."

And it sure did. I'll let you guess what came next.

For the next two days I stayed at her apartment. On Sunday evening, Pam drove me back to the base.

As I was getting out of the car I said, "You really know how to keep a promise."

She said to let her know when my next day off was. I promised her I would. As I was walking through the gate, the same MP who was on duty Friday night was on duty again. He asked if my girlfriend had a friend for him, and I told him I forgot to ask. I did see Pam again, and each time was better than the last. For the next few days my spirit was up and my mood was good. Then one night I got out a picture of Paula and read the letter about the divorce. I just needed to talk to her.

CHAPTER 18

July 1969

One day we got two new guys in our company. They had just returned from Vietnam, and now they were serving out the last eight months in the Army with us. One had gone to Vietnam as a PFC and the other a specialist E-4. They both returned as a sergeant E-5. They said that most guys made rank fast over there if you had the right Military Occupational Specialty (MOS). They both had been in the Army only three months longer than me and I was only a PFC. Their duty in Vietnam was driving convoys. They said at times there would be anywhere from fifty to seventy trucks in a convoy. They hauled everything including ammunition, construction material, combat rations, and pallets of other items needed for U.S. forces operating in Vietnam.

The situation between Paula and myself was still the same. I knew if I could just talk to her things would be different. I put in for a thirty-day leave, but I was turned down because I didn't have any leave time. I had used it all. I took ten days leave after Basic Training and just a day here and a day there. I would have to wait a year to accumulate any more leave. I could not wait that long.

The more I talked to the two new sergeants about Vietnam, the more I considered volunteering to go. I asked them a lot of questions about how bad it was over there. They said it all depended on your MOS and where you were stationed. They said some places were safer than others. They said the whole country was a war zone, but some GIs would never leave their base for the whole year they were there. They would get shot at by snipers and RPGs. For the most part when they didn't have any convoys, they were back in camp and didn't have KP duty because the Vietnamese Nationals were paid to do it. They made up for it with having a lot of guard duty, though. They also said you get some time for leave before going to Vietnam.

I had no mail that day from Paula, so I made up my mind to request a transfer to Vietnam. I walked into the Orderly Room one morning in July and asked for a 1049 Form.

The first sergeant came out of his office and said, "Are you sure about that?"

Everyone knew what a 1049 Form was. After telling the first sergeant about the situation I was having with Paula, he said that he understood and hoped she and I could work things out. He also said he hated losing a fine driver like me. The paperwork usually took about ten days to go through. I was scared about going. This might be difficult for some people to understand. Men were desperate to stay out of Vietnam, and here I was eager to go. I have never shared the fact with too many people that I volunteered to go to Vietnam. I just let them assume I had been ordered to the war.

The first sergeant was right—it only took ten days for my orders to come back. I was to leave two days later on July 28, with a stop at Fort Lewis, Washington, after my thirty-day leave. I was to go report to Fort Lewis on September 2. I was hoping to look up Carl while I was there. My first priority was trying to talk to Paula to see if we could work things out, though.

One Saturday in July when I had no KP or guard duty, and knowing I was leaving Monday, I requested a pass and went and gave Pam a call. She told me to be at the gate in ten minutes. After meeting Pam, we went back to her apartment and had a few beers and went for a swim. I told Pam that I had put in a transfer for Vietnam, and that I would be leaving on Monday. She said that she would miss me but she understood why I was doing it. We had one last night together that I never forgot.

CHAPTER 19

August 1969

After a short stop at Fort Dix for fuel and to let off some GIs and to pick up new ones, we were on our way to the Tulsa International Airport. We got into Tulsa at 11:30 pm, and I got the first taxicab back to Hominy. There were no lights on at the apartment, so I had the cab driver take me to my mother's house. She was still up and was very surprised by my visit. She put on a pot of coffee, and we talked for a very long time. Most of it was about Paula and the baby. She said the baby was doing just fine and was getting big. She told me she tried to talk to Paula about our situation, but all she could get out of her was that she didn't want to be tied down to just one person. She said she was too young to have gotten married.

That next day I went back to our apartment, and when Paula opened the door and saw me standing there, she almost fainted. She was not expecting me. I picked up the baby and played with him for a while until he got tired and went to sleep. Then Paula and I had a good long talk about everything, and I said I was hoping things would be better. For the next few weeks, things were fine between us. Or so I thought. We would ride out to the lake in the old '55 Chevy to our old spot and sit and talk for hours.

She said, "I still care for you, but I'm just not sure how much."

All I know is that I had done everything I knew to do. I told her I was going to Vietnam, and if she still felt the same when and if I got back, then she could have a divorce. To make this story short, after I got back from Vietnam, we did end up getting back together for about eighteen months. It just didn't work out any longer. In 1973, we got a divorce and I got full custody of our son.

Toward the end of August, I had to head back to Fort Lewis. My mother didn't know I was going to Vietnam. When I finally told her, she took it very hard. I told her about going to Fort Lewis and hoping to see Carl. She said to tell him that she loved and missed him. She said for me to be careful and to write her. She told me she would be praying for me to come back safe. She also said she would be praying for Paula and the baby.

The month of August went by so fast that it only seemed like I had been home for just a few days. I was hoping the months in Vietnam would go by just as fast. Only time would tell.

CHAPTER 20

September 1969—Fort Lewis, Washington

I arrived at Fort Lewis, Washington, late one night and checked in and was sent to some barracks for the night. Transient Barracks are usually the next thing to slum living. The building was cold, and we had no blankets or sheets. There were only a few bunks set up on the floor. The rest were disassembled or broken, and the mattresses were occupied with GIs lying on them. We were all awakened at 5:30 am the next morning by a little dick-faced corporal who thought he was a general. He told everyone to go for chow and to be back in one hour. After returning from chow, we were taken to this old building and issued Vietnam fatigues and jungle boots. The jungle fatigues were baggy with all sorts of pockets in them—four in the shirt and two huge ones on the sides of the trousers. They were great for carrying beer cans and other bulky items. The boots had thick rubber grips with the bigger part of the tops made out of canvas rather than leather for coolness.

After returning to the barracks, we prayed we would not get called for work detail. There was nothing like washing greasy dishes after a sleepless night right before heading to Vietnam. It does nothing for your morale. By this time, it was noon.

The same short, pimply, arrogant little dick-faced corporal came into the barracks and starting yelling: "You are to keep this barracks clean at all times! Everyone will be leaving here sometime tomorrow, so you are not allowed to leave here until then."

He turned and began walking away. I caught up to him and asked if I could go and try to find my brother since he was stationed here at Fort Lewis.

He said, "Didn't I just say no one was to leave the barracks?"

About this time, a sergeant E-6 who was going back to Vietnam with all of us told the dick-faced corporal to get lost. The corporal's face turned red as he walked away. The sergeant asked about Carl, and I told him that he got shot in Vietnam and that he's stationed in Fort Lewis for recovery. I told him I was hoping to see him before I left since it had been two years since I'd last seen him. He told me to go find Carl and not worry about the corporal—he would take care of him if he got me into any trouble.

He jokingly said, "What are they going to do anyways, send you to Vietnam for your punishment?"

I went and got Carl's address, and the sergeant wished me luck. I was about a block away when I stopped in front of this building with no kind of sign on it. I walked another two blocks then stopped a sergeant coming my way and showed him the address. He said it's back the other way. He said he was going to pass right by it and told me to join him. As it turned out, it was the building with no sign on it. I went inside and asked if I had the correct address. About this time, a group of soldiers came walking in. Some were using canes, some using two canes, and some sitting in wheelchairs. They were coming back from rehabilitation for their Vietnam wounds. At the end of the group was my brother, Carl, using a cane.

This PFC called out, "Sergeant Lott, you have a visitor."

Finally, Carl saw me and said, "What the hell are you doing here?"

He had no idea I was coming. After he got over the shock and surprise, we shook hands and gave each other a big hug.

Someone saw our nametags and asked Carl, "Sergeant Lott, is this your son?"

Carl then said, "Do I look old enough to have a twenty-year-old son, you dumbass?"

We talked some more and then left to go get a beer.

As we were leaving, Carl would tell everyone that we passed by, "This is my baby brother!"

We walked across the street to the NCO Club.

I said, "I can't go in there being only a PFC."

He said: "The hell you can't. You're with me, and they know better than to mess with us Vietnam vets."

We went inside, found a table, and Carl went and got a couple beers for us. As he was coming back, this sergeant E-6 was at the table telling me I was not allowed to be in there because of my rank. Carl walked up and asked the sergeant if he had a problem.

The sergeant said, "This PFC cannot be in here."

Carl said: "He is my younger brother and he leaves for Vietnam tomorrow. It's been two years since we've last seen each other. Have you been to Vietnam?"

The sergeant simply said, "No."

Then Carl said, "You had better turn around then and walk away if you know what's good for you."

A dozen or so other soldiers in the club came over to that sergeant and told him to get the hell out of there and reminded him that they were all Vietnam vets

Carl's medals, which include the Purple Heart and the Bronze Star

living in the same barracks as Carl. The sergeant did what he was told, nearly running out of the building.

For the next several hours, Carl and I talked and got caught up with each other about the last two years. During that time, neither Carl nor I had to pay for a single beer. The other Vietnam vets said that since Carl had stood up to that staff sergeant and because I was on my way to Vietnam, the beers were on them. Carl was walking pretty well now with the help of his cane.

I asked him when he was supposed to get back to his company, and he said: "Whenever I feel like it. We can come and go as we like. We have no duty. All we do is make morning formation and go to our rehabilitation two or three times a week, depending on our needs."

He told me that he had a permanent profile of no running, marching, jumping, or standing for over five minutes at a time until he gets out of the Army.

We talked about everything, aside from me going to Vietnam. I didn't tell Carl I had asked to go to Vietnam because I knew it would just hurt and disappoint him. I just let him assume that I got orders to go. Just before we left the NCO club, he tried to make me feel better by telling me the truck drivers in Vietnam had it really good. They got to ride instead of walk everywhere. He reminded me that infantry had to walk through the jungle. He assured me that I would be all right

Carl Lott, taken shortly before his death in 2011

and not to take any risks. He also told me not to trust any of the Vietnamese. He said that they can be your friend during the day and your enemy at night. He said the VC were everywhere, and they could very well be the barber who cuts your hair or the ten-year-old kid who asks to polish your boots. He said to be very careful wherever I went and whatever I did.

By this time it was getting late, and Carl said he was getting tired and his leg was beginning to bother him. I figured it had to do with all the beer he had drunk. He drank two beers for every one I did. He sure could drink that beer. I've never seen anyone who could drink as much as he could and not get drunk. We walked the short distance back to the Transient Barracks to find out what time I would be leaving the next day. We were told about 9:00 am. When Carl turned to leave, the same short, dick-faced corporal came over to me and asked if I had left the barracks, and I told him that I did. He said he was going to write me up for disobeying an order.

Carl then turned around, walked over to the corporal, and said: "Stand at attention, you little prick. If anyone gets written up, it'll be you. This is my brother, and he and the rest of these men are going to Vietnam, so piss off and get the hell out of here or I'll kick your ass and then write your sorry ass up for being such a dumbass. Now leave and don't mess with any of these men again."

Everyone in the barracks began clapping and yelling, and once again, the corporal's face turned red as he walked away as fast as his feet would take him. Carl said that he would be back in the morning to say goodbye.

The next morning at 9:00 am, we were put on the Army buses, OD green in color. I got the seat next to the window and began looking out for Carl. We started to pull away and I finally found him standing across the street. I waved, and then he came to attention and gave me a salute. As the bus picked up speed, I was hoping that I would be able to return his salute a year from then.

In July 2011, my brother Carl passed away from complications of Agent Orange. For the last few years of his life, he was receiving a hundred percent disability from the VA (Veterans Affairs). He was sixty-six years old. He had been awarded the National Defense Service Medal, the Vietnam Service Medal, the Vietnam Campaign Medal, the Good Conduct Medal, the Army Commendation Medal, the Bronze Star with the V for Valor, a Purple Heart, and the Combat Infantry Badge.

CHAPTER
21

The FNGs Are Here

In our new green jungle fatigues, we boarded a World Airline charter flight. After a twenty-two-hour flight, including refueling stops in Hawaii and Japan, we approached Cam Ranh Bay, South Vietnam, a little before dawn on September 7, 1969. And I thought the flight to Germany was a long one. Looking down on the lights of the base below us, I wondered if incoming planes were ever shot at. Did we have to run for cover when we left the plane? It struck me how little I really knew about the war, or the conflict, I was entering.

About this time, someone says, "Look at all those fireworks being set off."

The sergeant who was coming back for second tour of duty said: "Those are not the kind of fireworks you're thinking of, private. Those are mortars, rocket rounds, and artillery fire. Some unit down there is in a firefight."

Just prior to landing, the pilot came on the air to let us know where we were and give us the weather and ground conditions. The guy had a real sense of humor, depending on how you looked at it. He said, "Ground conditions consisted of light to scattered automatic weapons fire."

He said a couple other things that I don't remember. I just remember that they were designed to scare the crap out of us. So there we were, preparing ourselves right off for the worst.

It was a funny feeling descending the ramp onto Vietnamese soil. The ground conditions reported were completely false, but there were plenty of wary, wide-eyed soldiers leaving the plane, moving out only because they followed the soldier in front of them. I remember thinking to myself, *Here's to a year or however long I last.*

It was still dark in Cam Ranh Bay, and from first appearances, it looked like we had just made another stop at some airport completely unassociated with war, blood, and death. After a few moments, some flares popped off in the far outer perimeter area completely illuminating a hillside and wiggling down to their death like a flickering candle. In the far-off distance we could hear the sound of mortars and rockets. Right then I knew that it was no ordinary airport, and I stared apprehensively into the dark outside the secured areas.

Tired, uneasy, and awestruck, we were loaded onto buses and transported to the 22nd Replacement Battalion. As we boarded our buses, there were others being unloaded from theirs. They had skin that looked like brown leather shoes and bodies of those who had been on starvation diets for months. Their eyes were weary looking and their stares were cold. Most of them didn't say a word as they moved to board their "Freedom Bird."

A few, however, were vocal when they said things like: "The fucking new guys are here. You're going to love Nam."

You could tell the new guys from the veterans by their newly issued jungle fatigues, a grass-stain green with a yellowish tint. As they were washed and washed, they increasingly became a faded bluish green. Very old fatigues started to have a whitish tint with frazzled cuffs and seams. You could guess how long someone had been in-country by the shade of their fatigues. Since it's a status symbol of war, the more faded your fatigues, the more worthy one was.

The base was huge and barren. The oily pungency of shit burning, garbage rotting, and dead fish formed an aromatic combination that was standard Vietnam. The stifling heat and humidity were overpowering. We heard some small-arms fire in the distance the first evening we were there, and word spread among the newly arrived that a sniper had killed a perimeter guard.

Many of us believed that within the next few days we would be in the midst of a whole year of daily fighting for our lives. Bits of paper and trash littered the land, and the smell of piss, dung, and general poverty damn near made diesel fumes on our ride smell good. In addition, none of us had had a bath after leaving Fort Lewis about twenty-two hours back, so we were all beginning to smell ripe to each other, too.

Within twenty minutes, we arrived at the 22nd Replacement Battalion and got off the bus and moved into company formation. A sergeant began telling us that we would be at this company for about three to four days. During that time, we were told, we would be required to assemble in the open area three times each day beginning after chow to listen for our names to be called for orders and transportation to our new companies.

Within the assembly area were large wooden buildings with galvanized tin roofs. We were all ushered into one building with Army cots in them. After putting away our gear, we were taken to the Finance Office, where we were told to convert our American Dollars into Military Payment Certificates (MPCs). We were then instructed to write to our relatives explaining to them that we had arrived in South Vietnam. We were told to write the word "FREE" in the upper-right-hand corner of the envelope where the postage stamp would normally be affixed. All letters sent by us from Vietnam would be free of postage. Following our money exchange and letter writing, it was time to go to chow at the Mess Hall. We each were then told to go to our hooches (huts) and to remain there except for going to the outdoor toilets.

By this time it was near sundown, and we were learning how to use a mosquito net for the first time. None of us could go to sleep or stay asleep that first evening. No one talked very much to anyone around them either. We could hear small-arms fire and mortars that seemed to be maybe two miles or less away. I was worried but already getting a grip on reality. I was toughening myself for Vietnam.

After our sleepless night, the area became noisy around sunrise with the efforts of all to make it to the Mess Hall for breakfast. Leaving the Mess Hall, we could already hear the voice over the PA system announcing that the first formation for us in the yard would be at 8:00 am.

There was just enough time for everyone to use the latrines. We soon discovered that the showers were outdoors, made from huge rubber tanks atop wooden poles. We also discovered that the semi-tanker truck had not been around to put any water in them. The only water for use was in some small barrels, and they were for shaving only. The outdoor latrines were of two types. One for pissing was a pipe about eight inches in diameter that had been placed in a hole that was drilled for it at a considerable depth. There were many such "piss holes" to accommodate the hundreds of males in the area. The other latrines were for defecation. The "shitters" were wooden buildings with tin roofs about ten feet wide and twelve feet long with one entrance about thirty inches wide. On each side was a row of four crap holes with the toilet seats commonly used on porcelain stools. Below the lids were steel barrels that had been cut apart to provide the receptacle. On the outside of both sides of the building were four door flaps to remove the pots so they could be taken away to a spot where diesel fuel would be poured into them and set afire to make the pot once more ready for use. The latrines and their odors were everywhere, it seemed.

Our 8:00 am formation on our second day in-country was filled with little information and scant few assignments.

As we were about to turn and go back to our building, the PA system came on and said, "Will the following men come forward."

About nine names were called, mine being the last. The sergeant said that we ten men would be on guard duty that night. We were told to report to the large Supply Building at 6:00 pm and then be back here at 7:00 pm. After reporting to the Supply Building to get our gear, which consisted of a steel pot helmet, an M-14 rifle with two bandoliers of ammo, and a flak jacket, we all reported back to the sergeant at 7:00 pm, where a three-quarter-ton truck was waiting on us. The truck driver stopped at different locations where two men would get off. Another soldier and I were put on perimeter guard duty in bunkers somewhere on the base.

We settled into the sandbag bunkers and began to acquaint ourselves with the "old hands," or "old men" as we called them, on duty there. Those vets weren't really old—most of them were probably like myself, maybe twenty years old at the time. But they seemed old, especially to some of the men who were eighteen. They said that in the bush out there, "Charlie" already had a fix on our bunker position, and that he may or may not decide he wanted to open up with either rifle or mortar fire on us. It was our job to sit tight and be alert all night. If we were to light a cigarette, it had to be well below the sandbags where the light from the cigarette or lighter could not be seen. Near sunrise, after a long and boring night on guard, the bunkers shook with the hits of a few mortar rounds.

After guard duty, we made our way to the Mess Hall for breakfast, and it was already hot as hell early in the morning. Once outside the Mess Hall, I made my way back to the hooch. I unlocked my duffel bag I had padlocked to the springs next to the mattress with everything that belonged to me stuffed into it. I removed my shaving razor and shaving soap, and I was off to find some water in one of those outdoor showers that had water in its overhead tank. No such luck on the bath water, but there was some water for shaving at least. After returning to my hooch, I lay down on my Army cot. It was damn hot with no wind coming through the building, so I got up and pulled out my last cigarette from the pack.

The jet lag and change in climate were having their effect on me. I decided to go find the nearest PX. It was a mile or more away. Once there, I bought a carton of cigarettes, which sold for $1.10. I bought some food and snacks, too. I got a few cans of beer, which were $.10 a can. On the way back to my hooch, a two-and-a-half-ton truck stopped and asked if I would like a ride. The driver was a PFC, like myself, and he asked how long I had been in-country. I told him under a week. He said he had been there for three weeks and all he did was pick up new guys from the airbase and take the old guys leaving Vietnam to their Freedom Bird to go home. I asked him how he got such an easy job, and he said his father was a master sergeant in the Personnel Headquarters at Saigon. When his father knew he was coming to Vietnam at Cam Ranh Bay, he knew the right people to talk to. He asked what my MOS was, and I told him the same as his—a truck driver. We arrived at my hooch, and he stopped and told me good luck and was gone.

Soon after he dropped me off, I could see the water tanker truck making its rounds to the shower area. I found out the reason for no water in the showers: Snipers were taking potshots at the truck drivers and the MPs wouldn't let them on the road with the trucks until the snipers were taken care of. I went and got my toothbrush, a tube of toothpaste, a bar of soap, and a towel. I hurried to the shower area to take one long-ass shower.

The sun rose on my third day in Vietnam with the blasting volume of a radio station employee yelling out the greeting, "Good morning, Vietnam!"

The broadcast was compliments of the U.S. Armed Forces Radio Network. The radio played tunes by current artists, welcome to our ears. Whenever we were able to, soldiers in base camps all over Vietnam listened to that radio station.

After going to the Mess Hall, we all went to the morning formation, where about fifty names were called out for assignment. The formation following the noon meal produced orders for another fifty or so men. The same was true for the formation after the evening meal, until only about fifty of us, myself included, who seemed harder to assign for some reason, remained. By that time of day, another two hundred soldiers were arriving from the airbase for their tour of duty. That night as we sat on our cots drinking beer and playing cards and listening to the sound of artillery fire in the far-off distance, we were all thinking the same thing: Where will our fates take us?

At 8:00 am morning formation on my fourth day in Vietnam, my name was called out, "Lott, Nha Trang," along with twenty-five other soldiers and their destinations. The sergeant calling out our names said to get our gear and be back in one hour. At the formation area there was a large map of South Vietnam. All of us went to find the place called out with our names. There was even a few who had Cam Ranh Bay called out with their name, and they looked it up on the map, dumbasses. I found Nha Trang. It was north of Cam Ranh Bay and appeared to be about twenty miles away along the South China Sea. Within an hour we all were back with our gear. Two deuce-and-a-half-ton trucks were waiting on us. The sergeant in charge gave the order for everyone to begin climbing onto the trucks. He said we were going to the airbase to catch a ride to our new duty stations.

On the way, I was hoping and praying to get a safe place like the one we were just leaving behind. The soldiers at Cam Ranh Bay hardly ever left the base, a real REMF citadel. "REMF" is a term of derision used by front-line soldiers to describe those in cushy jobs in the rear. After we got out of the trucks at the airbase, names were being called out and men were put into groups depending on where they were going. Two other men and I were going to Nha Trang, and the rest were going to other places. The other men got onto planes. The three of us were put on a chopper. My first helicopter ride was exciting. The *whop-whop-whop* sound of the rotors had a captivating and calming sound that I loved. The countryside below, including the jungle and various small hamlets, was beautiful. Throughout my tour, I was struck by the beauty of the country, and sometimes I found it hard to believe that a war was going on. Each time I rode on a helicopter during my year, I never got over the thrill of them. To this day, the sound of a helicopter rotor, whether real or in a movie, stirs an excitement deep inside me.

With the three of us on the chopper, there were also two door gunners sitting with their legs hanging out the side of the chopper on each side, manning .50-caliber machine guns. We were in the air and headed north with the jungle on our left and the South China Sea on our right. Looking down at the jungle, I was thinking about my brother Carl and what he was thinking when they were on choppers being taken out and dropped off in the jungle, walking through the jungle and trying to find the VC day after day. I was really beginning to appreciate my MOS as a truck driver. As we approached the airbase at Nha Trang, I could see all kinds of military planes, helicopters, trucks, and even cars. The cars looked to be '66 Chevys with military OD-green paint. They were used for chauffeuring the officers around. Now that's the kind of job I would like to have.

From the air, Nha Trang looked to be more of a vacation spot, a picturesque tropical paradise outside of the war. Our chopper circled the airbase, landed, and out came a three-quarter-ton truck the three of us boarded. We drove away through a U.S. Air Force base that looked like it could have been transplanted lock, stock, and swimming pools right from the good old U.S.A.—except that the perimeters were close enough so that what was outside them told you the truth. The route we took carried us towards a bay and out off the airbase. We were on a road that paralleled the shore, a road we later knew well as just "Beach Road." It took us north, and on the right a couple hundred yards of beach filled the space between the road and the sea. It was a beautiful view, one that made it difficult to believe that a few miles in the opposite direction was blood, suffering, and death. On the left side of the road was an endless string of villas, half in disrepair, but all telling of past beauty.

On the road we followed, we met or passed other military vehicles of every size and description and several military personnel on foot. Flowing through the hubbub of military activity were the Vietnamese. These included the basket-laden pineapple-vendor ladies from the beach, a man, a woman, and two kids on a Honda 50 weaving through traffic, prostitutes calling out, "I suck you, $5.00, you number-one GI," and kids in packs surrounding walking soldiers and relieving the unwary of anything on them that wasn't nailed down. Heading the other direction was a Jeep with two MPs sitting in the front and another sitting in the back holding onto a mounted M-60 machine gun. Following the Jeep was one of those OD-green 1966 Chevy sedans. On the front license plate were three stars, meaning inside was a lieutenant general. Following the sedan was another Jeep with MPs and another mounted M-60 machine gun. I was thinking what a lucky guy the driver was, and how does a soldier get a job like that.

After a half-mile of driving, we made a left turn onto a compound that was a replacement company, and I was thinking this was going to be my permanent duty station. We were told to dismount the truck with our gear and after our names were crossed out to check with forward orders and to grab a bunk in the lower-level open bay of the barracks. I figured I had finally reached the end of my immediate traveling, but it was not to be at this time. There were so many men coming and going, some wearing faded fatigues and some, like myself, wearing very new ones. I felt out of place. I felt like trying to find a pair of old fatigues so I wouldn't stand out so much.

It was around 6:00 pm when a buck sergeant came into the hooch and said: "I need six men for guard duty. Do I have any volunteers?"

No one volunteered so he picked out six of us. I was thinking, *I have only been in-country for five days, and this will be my second guard duty.*

After being issued our rifles and two bandoliers of ammo, we were loaded into a three-quarter-ton truck and driven to our assigned guard stations. My guard post was on the far backside of the base, where the base and jungle meet with rolls and rolls of barbed wire separating the two. A guard tower about twenty-five-feet tall would be my place of duty. The sergeant of the guard said that the area to our front was a free-fire zone, and that we could fire on anything or anyone without getting permission first. As I began to climb the tower, he said someone would be coming by every half-hour or so to check on things. About three hours into my guard duty, I could hear in the far-off distance the sound of small weapons firing in the direction of a very large mountain to my west. A few minutes later, about six or seven helicopters left the airbase and headed in the direction of the mountain. Soon after, the night sky looked like a Fourth of July fireworks show back home, except this one was the difference between life and death.

The helicopters were spreading fire on what seemed to be the base of the mountain with their M-60 machine guns, with every fifth round being a tracer round. It looked like a spring of fire going back and forth. After about ten or fifteen minutes, the firing stopped and the helicopters returned to base. I was thanking God that I was watching where I was instead of out there being a part of it. The sergeant of the guard arrived around this time and asked how I liked the show. He said about a dozen of Fifth Special Forces soldiers had walked into an ambush of VC units. They called in a dust-off for two WIAs.

The next morning I was awakened by what seemed like every radio in Vietnam with the blasting volume sound of "Good morning, Vietnam!" The guy on the radio said that today's temperature would be hot, hot, and hotter. The disk jockey said to be careful because Mr. Charlie was everywhere. I got up and headed for a shower and then went to the Mess Hall, where the food was a lot better than that at Cam Ranh Bay. The sergeant said I would be here one more day but not to leave the area. I went back to the hooch, and I could hear a few guys being put on some kind of detail. I didn't want any part of that, so I left to find the EM Club and have a few beers. I then walked across the road to the beach and found a spot to sit and drink my beer. Crossing the road was like taking your life in your own hands.

In no time, I was approached by a young Vietnamese girl.

She said, "GI, you make love to me, $5.00."

I said, "No, thanks."

As she was walking away, she turned and said: "You number-ten GI. Number ten is a bad number to the Vietnamese."

I then was off to find the trucking company where I was hoping to be stationed, but I found out it was too far a walk. There were so many Vietnamese coming and going, I began to wonder how many of them were VC. By now it was close to chow time and I was getting hungry.

As I was sitting and eating, this guy I had gone through Basic Training with came over and asked, "Didn't we go through Basic together at Fort Ord?"

I said, "I believe we did."

He asked how long I had been in Vietnam and if I was stationed here at Nha Trang. I told him that I was just waiting to be assigned to a duty station, and that I had only been in-country for a few days. I told him I was hoping to get stationed here at the truck company. He said he knew someone who could make that happen. He said that his boss, a specialist E-7 in the Personnel Office, had the authority to do almost anything, and that he owed him a favor. He said he would check on my orders and let me know later. After we got caught up on things for the past year or so, he wrote down my full name and service number and then left. I went back to my hooch.

About an hour later, he came back to my hooch and said that everything was taken care of, but it would take a few days for my paperwork to go through.

He said that if I was sent to another base not to worry because I would be back here in no time. His name was Scott Sawyer, specialist fifth class. He'd been in Vietnam for ten months. He came over as a PFC and made E-4 in two weeks, then made E-5 just two weeks before. I was beginning to find out that it always paid to know the right person.

The next morning, as we were gathering and waiting on our orders for our duty stations, Scott came walking up. About this time someone on the PA speaker started calling out names with their duty station.

My name was called out near the end, "Lott, Tuy Hoa."

Scott told me that Tuy Hoa was about sixty miles north, about a two-hour drive by truck or thirty minutes by chopper. The PA speaker said to be back in one hour with gear, prepared to leave for our duty station. Scott said not to worry, I would be back here in less than two days. He said Tuy Hoa was a very small base and he sure as hell would not like to spend a year there. Scott said he had to get to work, but to come by and see him when I got back. We said our good-byes, and I left to get my gear. I was sure hoping Scott knew what he was talking about.

One hour later we were on our way to the airbase to catch a chopper to Tuy Hoa. Three choppers were waiting for us with rotor blades turning. There were five men to each chopper. I climbed onto the third one with four others. These were the same-looking choppers with door gunners sitting, legs hanging out the side, manning .50-calibers. The three choppers rose and headed north along the coast. There is nothing like riding in a chopper and hearing the blades make the unmistakable sound. To this day, I can hear a chopper far off in the distance before others can around me. Whenever I hear a chopper today, I have to stop whatever I'm doing and look up. Memories of Vietnam always come rushing back.

After about twenty minutes, the choppers left the coastline and turned left, heading inward into the jungle of thick tangled masses of tropical vegetation. We soon came to a clearing about fifty yards by fifty yards wide.

As the choppers started to descend, we could see purple smoke coming from the clearing with men standing at the edge of the jungle holding their weapons and waving their arms. I began thinking, *Oh shit, is this where I'm going?*

The men on the other two choppers jumped off, leaving me and one other soldier on board. I found out later that those men were in the infantry and were replacements. I was so thankful to still be on the chopper. I said a few silent thank yous to God. We continued our flight to the Tuy Hoa airbase. From the air, I could tell I didn't like the place. It was nothing like Nha Trang.

After we landed, the other soldier and I got off the chopper, where a PFC came up to us and said: "Welcome to Tuy Hoa. Get your gear and come with me."

We followed him to a Jeep and after loading our gear, we drove off the airbase and onto a road—if that's what you want to call it. The "road" was very rough with holes all over, making the ride bumpy as hell. There was not a smooth spot to be found. Both sides of the road were barren of any vegetation. Swirling red dust was everywhere. The smell was damn awful. Latrines, shit burning, rotting garbage, and dead fish. Still the Vietnam standard. The stifling heat and humidity were overpowering. If things were not bad enough, a U.S. Air Force plane was flying a short distance from us, spraying that heavy red substance. As the wind picked up, it brought it over us. Our fatigues became covered with the red spray. I was trying to cover my nose and mouth. We were coughing and choking and cussing. *Dumbass Air Force people.*

The driver said the red spray was Agent Orange, but it wasn't harmful to soldiers. I called bullshit. If it can kill vegetation, then it couldn't be good for humans.

We began to meet and pass Vietnamese people on their motorcycles, small cars, and trucks. A convoy of trucks with an MP Jeep both in front and behind the convoy passed us going in the other direction. These MP Jeeps had a machine gun mounted behind the driver with a soldier manning it. As we drove through the front gate of the Tuy Hoa Army Base, a U.S. Army MP and a South Korean MP waved us through. Razor-sharp barbed wire about five feet tall lined both sides of the road. The road went up and around to the top of a hill, where the driver pulled up to a large wooden building with a galvanized tin roof and screen-wired windows, with about four feet of sandbag walls for protection. The sign out front read "Headquarter and Headquarter Company" and other things I cannot recall. Across the road were two large buildings with a large white sign that read "South Korea, White Horse Division," with a big white horse painted on it.

The driver told us to go inside and give our orders to the company clerk and then he left. As we were giving our orders to the clerk, the first sergeant walked in and asked which of us was PFC Lott. I told him that was me, and then he asked the clerk for my orders. After checking my orders he said there was some kind of mixup back in Nha Trang. He said I would be going back there tomorrow. On the inside I was smiling my ass off because I knew I would not like this place at all. He told the other soldier that he was the new company Jeep driver, and that he would be taking the place of the soldier that picked us up this morning. He said that he's going home in a few days.

We were taken to a hooch and found some empty cots. I was feeling so good about going back to Nha Trang that I had a hard time going to sleep that night. I finally got to sleep around 2:30 am and woke up having to take a piss. As I was walking over to the pissing hole, all hell broke loose, an incoming VC rocket landing on the hooch I had just left a few minutes before. My first thought was to run to the nearby bunker. But my instinct told me to go to the hooch and help the men inside if I could. About this time, in a matter of a few seconds, another rocket hit the company Jeep that was parked nearby. By then, men were running all over the area to their guard positions. I went over to the hooch, where someone was yelling out in what sounded like a lot of pain. Other men showed up and started helping the injured with their wounds. Of the fifteen men in the hooch, only five had wounds and only one of them was a serious wound, to the head. I looked over to this one guy as he pulled out a knife and ran it across his left arm, but only enough to let out a little blood. I asked him what he was doing. He said he would get a Purple Heart for his wound. I told him he was nuts. The two rockets were all we got from the VC that night.

I stayed in the bunker the rest of the night. I was so thankful I would be going back to Nha Trang in the morning. I didn't sleep the rest of the night. As soon as I got back, I was planning on looking up Scott Sawyer and buying him a beer.

Just past noon the next day, I got a chopper going back to Nha Trang. As I was getting off the chopper, there was Sawyer. He was going on R&R for the next seven days. He asked how I liked Tuy Hoa, and I said it sucked big time. I told him about getting hit with the rockets, and I thanked him for getting me back here to Nha Trang. He said that it was no problem, and that after he got back from R&R I could buy him that beer.

After being in-country for a week, I finally was going to my new company, the 10th Logistical Support Group South. The driver of the Jeep that was taking me to my unit pulled out of the Air Force Base and asked what I thought of Vietnam, how long I had been in the Army, and where I came from back in the real world. He told me he had been in-country for ten months. He talked all the way back to our unit. I hardly got to say a word. The drive from the air base took us along the beach, south for about two miles, until we arrived at what would be my home for the next eight months. The last four months of my tour of duty will be another story. The drive along the beach was one beautiful ride. It was hard to tell a war was going on just a few miles away. I came to love the beach when I could get a day off.

After reporting in and giving my orders to the company clerk, I was told to get a cot in one of the hooches. I found a cot, made my bed, got the mosquito net spread over the top of it, got my gear put away, and was off to the Mess Hall. The food was the best I had had since being in-country. After chow, I was off to find the PX and pick up a few things I needed. On the way back to the hooch, I noticed many Vietnamese walking around the company area. Some old Vietnamese men were picking up small rotten fish lying on some large rocks. I found out later that was their way of preparing the fish to eat. It smelled bad.

The Vietnamese women were carrying what seemed to be dirty jungle fatigues. As I walked into my hooch, a young girl maybe around seventeen or eighteen years old was sitting on the floor with at least a dozen pairs of jungle boots around her. She had half of them polished to a nice shine. I went over to her and said hello. She said in her Vietnamese language that her name was Lynn. I found out she was one of the hooch maids. She would come to work every day except Sunday at 7:00 am to wash our laundry, shine our boots, and clean the hooch for $5.00 per man a month. In our hooch, there were fifteen men. At $5.00 each, Lynn would make $75.00 a month. That was a lot of money in 1969 for a Vietnamese person. Lynn was very pretty. She was small with dark almond-shaped eyes and long black hair. She moved gracefully in her national dress of long trousers under a long-sleeved tunic slit from hem to waist. One could see some sign of French ancestry in her face. Lynn was very quiet and polite. I came to admire her for her hard work, her attitude, and how she would not give in to some of the guys when they were trying to have sex with her.

There were ten hooches with about fifteen men in each hooch. Each hooch had its own hooch girl. There was five hooches in a row on one side and fives hooches on the other side with a walkway in between. All of the hooches had four- or five-foot-tall sandbag walls around them. Between each hooch were bunkers with sandbags all around and on top. I would see the inside of those bunkers a lot over the months to come.

After settling in, I sat on my cot writing a letter to Paula to give her my address when some of the men came into the hooch after getting off duty. I say "off duty," but in Vietnam you really were on duty twenty-four hours a day, not knowing when an incoming rocket might hit or when a sniper decided to take a shot at someone. As the men came into the hooch, they came over and introduced themselves. They were all either PFCs or specialist E-4 pay grades. About this time, a guy walked in who would become my best friend in Vietnam. He walked over to the bunk next to mine and introduced himself. His name was Ray but said everyone called him Moose. I asked him how he got the name Moose, and he said when he was ten years old, he and his dad went moose hunting and he shot his first moose, so his dad just started calling him that. The bunk he came over to was his. He asked how long I had been in-country, and I told him about a week. He said that he got in the first week of July. We talked for a while and then he asked if I would like to go to the EM Club for a beer. The EM Club was only a short walk.

At the club, we got a table and ordered two beers. The place was pretty nice. You could order hamburgers, French fries, tea, soda pop, and mixed drinks. A big ceiling fan helped move the hot air around. Moose said that though the EM Club had a ceiling fan, the Officer's Club had air conditioning. While I was 5'10" and weighed one hundred forty-five pounds, Moose was 6'0" and about two hundred forty-five pounds. After a half dozen beers, I was feeling pretty good. I found out that Moose could out-drink anyone and still never get drunk. There was a raised platform where bands from the Philippines and other countries made attempts to sound like the current American musicians. For some reason, there was no band playing that night. Moose was a very quiet guy. He wasn't one to draw any attention to himself, not one to get upset very easily. But when he did get upset, you had better get out of his way, as I was to find out later.

Moose said I should like it here because we hardly ever had formation. Each day our next day's assignment was posted on a bulletin board in front of the Orderly Room. It was usually which truck you would be driving and what time you would be leaving the base and where you would be going. There was no KP duty because the Vietnamese do all the KP for a price. We did have to pull guard duty and fill sandbags and other small things when we were not on convoys. But mainly our job was to haul cargo. We would get sniper fire, so we had to be alert at all times. There were two guys on each truck, a driver and someone riding shotgun. It was our responsibility to check the bulletin board every day. It was getting close to chow, so we left. After chow, we went back to our hooch, where you could hear someone playing rock 'n' roll music and someone playing country.

The next day was Sunday, and we had no duty so we got a ride to the beach. It was already hot by the time we arrived at the beach. We swam for about an hour and then got a ride back and went to the EM Club again. Moose said Nha Trang was a REMF paradise. I agreed with him. About this time, two men came in who were friends of Moose. They sat down at our table and began telling us how bad they had it. One of them was a driver for a major. He drove one of those staff sedan cars. He said he picked up the major at 6:00 am in the morning to take him back to his hooch and now he was off duty for the day. The other guy said he had to pick up his colonel at 9:00 am in the morning and take him to the beach so he could swim for an hour. Then he had to take him back to his hooch, and then it took an hour to get sand out of the car. Moose looked at the two and told them they should be truck drivers because we're the ones who have it easy. Then he looked my way and winked. After they left, Moose said it must be hard to be a REMF in a war zone. He said he wondered if they would tell their families how bad they had it over here after they got back home.

After getting back to our hooch, we went to check the bulletin board for the next day. I was to ride shotgun with Moose. I was glad it was him and not someone else. I went over to the Supply Room to draw an M-16 rifle, steel-pot helmet, flak jacket, and a couple bandoliers of ammo for the convoy that next morning. At 6:00 am, we left our base in a ten-truck convoy. Moose and I were the third truck in line. Depending on how many trucks were in the convoy, we would draw numbers to see where we would be in line. Nobody liked to be the first truck because that's the truck that was most likely to run over any land mines the VC placed on the ground to destroy the truck and probably kill the men inside. Moose told me that on a convoy last month, the lead truck had run over a mine and blew the engine out of the truck. The driver and the guy riding shotgun had to be medivacked by chopper to the hospital back at Nha Trang and then to the hospital in Japan and then back to the States. He said he never heard any more about their condition. I was beginning to get nervous about this whole convoy thing.

Our convoy route ran west, some ten miles to an Infantry Base Camp and then southeast for another five miles to another Infantry Base Camp. We were taking them ammunition, construction material, water, food, mail, and pallets of other items needed for U.S. forces operating in the middle of Vietnam.

On our return trip, we would stop at three different villages to distribute some food and building material, such as four-by-eight galvanized tin sheeting the Vietnamese loved to get to build their one-room hooches. And we always had candy for the kids. The roads were very rough, and we could drive no faster than twenty or twenty-five miles per hour. The roads were more of paths through the jungle. Our clothes became dirty real fast from the dust kicked up by the truck in front of us. It took no time for our clothes to become soaked from the heat of Vietnam. With our MP Jeep escort in front and back of our convoy and the gunship flying overhead, we headed back to Nha Trang.

The first thing everyone did after getting back was take a very long shower. We had to get out of the dirty, sweaty clothes. The day had gone by fast with my first convoy in Vietnam. I had been expecting to get shot at by a sniper at any time, but on this day we did not have any problems with the VC. The adrenaline rush was a new high I would get each time we were on convoy. After chow, I went to check the bulletin board. There would be no convoy the next day, but Moose, a few other guys, and I were on shit-burning duty. The good part about burning shit was that it only took about half a day and then we were free to do as we pleased.

We pulled the steel barrels out and away from the wooden buildings, then poured diesel into the barrels and set them on fire. Every so often we had to stir the barrels and mix in more diesel fuel and reset the fire. The stench from the mixture of fumes was enough to make you throw up, which I did on more than one occasion.

On the morning of September twenty-eighth, I was called into the Orderly Room and the first sergeant gave me my promotion orders for specialist E-4 pay grade.

CHAPTER
22

October 1969

We had no convoys for over a week now. When I say no convoys, I mean Moose and I didn't have any. Every day a convoy would go out, but if your name was not on the bulletin board, then you were put on one of the Army's many other details. Moose and I had no convoy duty for over a week, and we were getting tired of pulling guard duty, burning the shit, and filling sandbags. It seemed like we were always filling sandbags for whatever reason. One night, Moose, some of the other guys, and I were out sitting on our bunker drinking beer, smoking some weed, and watching an artillery unit fire rounds onto the mountain west of us. They would do this any time of the day or night to let the VC know we were keeping an eye on them. The artillery rounds were landing all over that mountain, which looked to be only a few miles away. They were putting on one heck of a show. It was a sight I would never forget. The ground would shake with every explosion. All of a sudden we could hear small-arms fire not too far away. We all jumped off the bunker and ran to our hooch to get our rifles. Everyone was thinking we were under attack. I was asking myself if I could actually kill another person, even if it was the enemy.

The small-arms fire was becoming closer to our area. The alert warning signal was going off. The ground was shaking from the artillery hitting the mountain. The wailing warning-alert whistle and the small-arms fire made it scary. I am not ashamed to say, I was getting a little scared. Okay, a whole lot scared. After about fifteen minutes, the small-arms fire stopped and the all-clear whistle went off.

Moose asked me later if I had been scared, and I said, "How do you think my pants got wet?"

We found out later a soldier had gotten a "Dear John" letter. He was stressed out over it so he took a Jeep and was riding around firing his M-16 into the air. They said he emptied over twenty clips of ammunition. Thank goodness no one was injured. We went back to drinking our beer, thankful it was not the real thing. The next day was Sunday, and Moose and I had no duty so we decided to go to the beach. It was 9:00 am in the morning and the temperature was already over a hundred degrees. This would be my first time going to the Nha Trang beach. As soon as we found a spot, these Vietnamese girls came over and tried to get us to leave with them. The war made more prostitutes out of these girls because the money was an easy way to provide for their families, and the soldiers were young and horny. When you have eighteen-, nineteen-, and twenty-year-old men around these girls of the same age, sex is bound to happen. We told these girls no and to leave us alone. We went from being called "Number One GI" (a good number in Vietnam) to being called "Number Ten GI" (a very bad number in Vietnam).

After a while we decided to go back to our compound and get cleaned up and go to chow, then get a ride to downtown Nha Trang. This would be my first time downtown. As soon as we left the gates to our compound, we hailed a lambretta, a Vietnamese version of a taxi—a motorized three-wheeled affair. It was a miniature pickup with tiny wheels built for the smaller Asian people. The top speed was about thirty to forty miles per hour. We putted downtown in this modern-day rickshaw, paid the driver $2.00, and headed off to Luc's Bar. Moose had been there once before, so I just tagged along as he searched for the right street. As I trudged along, I took a good look around me. Nha Trang was by population one of the larger cities of Vietnam. There were motorcycles, motorbikes, bicycles, lambrettas, rickshaws, and MP Jeeps all over the place. There was mud, sewage, trash, and odors of every description everywhere. Flies, of course, were attracted to it all. It was common to see the Vietnamese squatting to relieve themselves. The sewage drained out into the streets. The houses in this part of Nha Trang were no more than chicken coops by our standards. They were maybe ten by twenty feet. The general construction material here appeared to be a combination of stucco and cement with galvanized tin on the roof. It was a little bit spooky walking through this area. The VC were frequently in Nha Trang, and it was quite possible to get wiped out in some back street where there was no immediate help. VC looked like everyone else. We drew a lot of stares.

We finally found Luc's Bar. It measured approximately ten by twenty feet and had no common walls with other abodes. Mrs. Luc invited us to sit down at the table near the entrance. Just as we sat down, the girls came over and asked us to buy them a "Saigon Tea." Sex was a readily available commodity in Nha Trang, and it was packaged and marketed in every imaginable way and sold in some form on half the streets of the city. It was not just the sexual acts that brought in hard cash. It was the anticipation that brought in even more. Soldiers spent hundreds of dollars buying the bar girls Saigon Tea, shot glasses filled with coke. It was $2.00 a shot, and it came with a girl fondling the solider, with the soldier returning the favor, while he harbored the illusion of having sex with her. If it wasn't Saigon Tea, it was PX goods GIs bought for the girls with the idea of getting sex in return. The girls then would sell the goods on the black market for the cash. The profit from these and the alcohol consumed all revolved around and existed because of sex.

The lambretta and rickshaw business surely benefited, for example, from ferrying horny GIs downtown and back. Sex was so obtainable and so inexpensive that it was next to free. The GI dollar was big and difficult to pass up. I indulged, and though I don't feel particularly guilty, I suppose in the end I am as guilty as all the others. I hope those who read this will understand the reasons for writing this story. There is no changing what has happened, and not telling it like it was would leave out a big part of my tour of duty in Vietnam. Anyone who was not there should be hesitant to judge too quickly. We were young—eighteen-, nineteen-, twenty-year-old young men—and our arteries flowed with the urges of hormonal youth. This and the fact that it was not ridiculous to think you might not make it back home. My intentions were good. When I arrived, I had no plans to participate, both out of respect for my wife and for the fear of getting a disease. I didn't know then that I'd be stationed at some place like Nha Trang, where it was available every day of the week for my entire tour. If you liked to drink and party a little, you eventually came into contact with a prostitute.

I was at Nha Trang only two weeks when I was first dared into trying out the steam bath and massage parlor on our compound near the bars. It was more affectionately known by the GIs as a "steam and cream" shop. The services offered were a soothing steam bath, a massage by a female employee, and a grand finale of your choice by the same employee. The price was 200 piastre, the equivalent to $2.00.

Back at Luc's Bar, Moose and I were feeling no pain with all the beer we had consumed. A soldier in the bar was giving one of the bar girls a hard time and making an ass of himself. Mrs. Luc told him to leave, and he said he was not leaving until the girl gave him what he had paid for, which was a blow job. The girl said he did not pay for one. The soldier got the girl by her hair and began to pull her down. Moose got up and walked over to the guy and told him to leave. The guy took a swing at Moose and missed. Moose gave the guy a short upper cut and the guy was out cold. We hailed a taxi and told the driver to take the guy back to the compound. Mrs. Luc was very thankful for the help from Moose and said he could have any one of the girls for free. Moose said maybe next time because we also had to leave.

We got back to the compound just in time for evening chow. After chow, we went over to the bulletin board, and our names were finally there for an eight-truck convoy to Ninh Hoa, some place north of Nha Trang along the coastline on

Highway One, the main road that ran north and south. Moose said that this was one of the best roads in Vietnam. The VC kept blowing it up, and the engineers kept fixing it. He said to be alert at all times for an ambush, though.

We arrived the next morning at our trucks with an MP Jeep up front with its M-60 machine gun mounted behind the driver with three MPs in the Jeep. The eight trucks were lined up behind the Jeep, and at the back of the trucks was another Jeep with the M-60 mounted on it with another three MPs—a driver, a person riding shotgun, and one manning the M-60. This time, Moose would be driver and I would ride shotgun. Coming back, we would trade places. Ninh Hoa was twenty-five miles away, about one-and-a-half-hour's drive in a convoy. About half an hour driving time down the highway we began to meet and pass Vietnamese people on their motorcycles, small cars, and trucks. The force of air coming in through the windows was hot and very uncomfortable. By 10:00 am, the temperature was already ninety-five degrees. Along the sides of the highway, we began to see large signs painted on four-by-eight-foot sheets of plywood. The signs had a white background with large red letters that read, in English, "CAR WASH." Moose said that these roadside businesses were not car washes. The business that was performed was prostitution. The young women sometimes stood by the road sign and held smaller cardboard signs that read "CAR WASH" to lure the GIs off their journeys for quick sexual acts. The medics advised us that the safest sex with Vietnamese women was the "hand job." U.S. soldiers in Vietnam were constantly informed about venereal diseases.

A few miles from Ninh Hoa, our convoy passed over a bridge. On the bridge were the bodies of four dead VC. Their black, swollen, stinking bodies had been left there for three days as a lesson to any future sabotage attempts. Bridges were always a target for the VC. The Army of the Republic of Vietnam (ARVN) and U.S. forces did everything they could to keep the bridges safe. We pulled through the gate to the Ninh Hoa Base and into an area where the trucks would be unloaded of their cargo, all except for one. This one truck's cargo was to go to a village on our way back to Nha Trang.

While waiting on the trucks to be unloaded, the drivers went to the EM Club to have a few beers. As we were drinking our beers, incoming mortar rounds hit the far side of the base. There were only two rounds but it was enough to keep everyone alert. The mortar was only harassment from Charlie Viet Cong to piss everyone off. We got our gear, went back to the trucks, and left toward the village for our next stop. The village was off Highway One down a rural and rugged road through the thick tangled mass of tropical vegetation. The drive was hard, and we were bouncing up and down, our heads hitting the roof of the truck. Just as we approached the outskirts of the village, we began to receive sniper fire. The guys riding shotgun opened up with their M-16 rifles on full automatic, firing into the jungle at anything that moved. The MP Jeeps were firing their M-60s. We didn't know if we had shot or wounded anyone, and we didn't take the time to find out. The convoy drove right past the village and didn't stop until we reached Highway One. After stopping and inspecting the trucks, we found a few holes in the side of three of the trucks. Moose and I found two holes just above the front tire on my side of our truck. Moose had used up four magazines of ammo as he rode shotgun.

We arrived back at Nha Trang very tired and very tense from being shot at and miserable from the oppressive heat, choking dust, and the unbelievably potholed roads. Whether I was driving or riding shotgun, it was always very unnerving. After taking a nice long hot shower and putting on some clean clothing and going to the Mess Hall to eat, we were off to the EM Club for a beer. That night a rock band from Australia put on a great show for us. The group was surprisingly good, singing most of the current favorite tunes that we all knew and liked. Besides the band, there were three go-go girls wearing tight nylon body suits and of course that went over well with the guys. With the beer and weed in our systems, some of the guys were feeling no pain as the group played song after song while the girls danced on stage. Toward the end of the show, a young blonde stripper appeared and her act came close to causing a riot. Everyone at the show seemed to enjoy the brief respite from the war. I know I sure did. After the singing of the Animals' hit song "We Gotta Get Out of This Place," the show ended. The men gradually drifted back to their hooches and crashed on their cots, tired and full of beer.

What a day it turned out to be. After a long day of driving in the hot oppressive heat of Vietnam and being shot at and then after a night of drinking beer and looking at pretty girls, I began to think of how crazy this place was. I now have been in Vietnam for two months with another ten to go.

CHAPTER 23

November 1969

The second week of November, Moose and I had gone to the Medivac Hospital to visit a friend who had an emergency hernia operation the day before. After leaving him, we stopped at the EM Club for some drinks. We stayed there a couple of hours, getting pretty high and enjoying a Vietnamese band who did a great job on the Beatles' "Hey Jude." Or maybe we just had too many beers to tell the difference. As we left the club into the bright and hot sun, we could hear the dull thuds of rotating helicopter blades, like a rapid, timed, synchronized rug beating. They reached a point directly over the Medivac Hospital, hovering within the designated area to land. There were two choppers, each carrying two wounded soldiers, one on either side of the chopper, strapped horizontally to a stretcher on the outside. They were bloody and mangled, dark red on their fatigues and field dressings. There was no movement from two of them, but the others emitted groans and some motion. I stood in horror, fear, and a degree of shock. It affected me deeply as it does today, every time I see a chopper.

God only knows where and what kind of hell these men went through out in the boonies. One second you are drinking beer, laughing, and having a good time forgetting there's a war going on, and the next second, the cold reality of it all hits you right in the face. As we turned to leave, the two choppers took off and two more were waiting to land with more wounded soldiers. We got back to our hooches to find out that two of our friends had gotten an early-out by thirty days. They would be leaving the next day. We were greeted with yells, applause, and laughter as we walked into the hooch. We were happy for them but at the same time we hated to see them go. We hated to see all of our friends go because we knew that it would be unusual if we ever saw these guys again. Some fellows you got to know really well and lived a short life with them that only they knew about and understood. Only under unusual circumstances would it ever be re-lived. When friends left, it sealed off forever a time and an important phase of your life. The guys you knew best were there when you got there, and you got to watch every one of them leave. We drank beer and talked with them until late into the night.

The next morning Moose, a few of the guys, and I drove the two men to the airbase and said our goodbyes. On the way back to the compound, we made a stop at the Medivac Hospital to see our friend. He was getting ready to come back to our compound but would be on light duty for the next ten days. He told us the men we saw being brought in by the choppers yesterday had been in a firefight. About two dozen VC had walked into an ambush the GIs had set up. They killed sixteen and wounded another five of the VC before a few had gotten away. Our guys had two KIAs and five WIAs.

So far this month, I have been on guard duty five times, burned shit four times, filled sandbags four times, and went out on convoys eleven times. It's now the end of November with nine more months to go in Vietnam.

CHAPTER 24

December 1969

December in Vietnam and the temperature at 7:00 am was already in the nineties. Back in Oklahoma, the average temperature is typically in the forties and fifties this time of year. Moose, some other guys, and I had sandbag duty, so we got a truck from the motor pool and drove to the beach and filled sandbags all morning. As we tried to leave the beach, our truck became stuck in the sand. The more the wheels turned, the deeper the tires became stuck. We started throwing off sandbags until we had enough off so the truck could get unstuck. We got back to the compound and unloaded the sandbags and went back for the rest of them. When we got back to the beach, there was another truck with guys putting our sandbags into their truck. They were from an Air Force company. We told them the sandbags were ours. They told us to get fucked. That's all it took for Moose to jump on two of them by himself. The fight was on, but it didn't last long because MPs showed up and put an end to it. We told them what happened, but the Air Force guys got to keep our sandbags. We had to spend another two hours filling new sandbags.

When we arrived back at the company area, I was notified I would be pulling guard duty that night for another soldier who had an accident of some kind. I reported later and found out I had perimeter guard duty. That's where the guards had to walk up and down the barbed wire in full view under the lights that illuminated the perimeter. No one cared for this kind of guard duty because if the VC wanted something to shoot at, you would be the easiest target in all the light. I never did understand why the Army had soldiers walking around at night in an area that was lit up like a football field in the middle of a war zone. I had to walk from one light back to the other, which were about a hundred yards apart. About halfway between the lights was somewhat of a dark spot. After about ten minutes in the bright light, I had the feeling that someone was observing my every move. I decided to stop at a dark spot and sat down so I would be somewhat out of sight. The area on the other side of the wire was a free-fire zone. Anything or any person that moved could be shot at on the spot.

About two hours into my watch, I could hear the faint sound of someone talking on the other side of the wire in what sounded like Vietnamese. I put my M-16 on full automatic and took the safety off. I was ready to pull the trigger. The talking stopped for about five minutes and then it started up again. This time it seemed to be closer and more to the right of where it last was. I was lying on the ground now, very still. I was hoping the sergeant of the guard would show up as it was time for him to make his rounds. If the VC were out there, I could not understand why they had not seen me. Good luck on my part, I guess. The noise was getting louder. I took half of my magazines of ammo and laid them on the ground beside me, thinking it would be faster to get to them that way. I said it's now or never so I pulled the trigger. I was sweeping the area back and forth. I emptied three magazines and was waiting on the VC to open up but nothing happened. In fewer than five minutes, the sergeant of the guard and the MPs showed up with a very bright spot light. I told them what I had heard. They checked the other side of the wire and found some blood but no body. The base was put on alert the rest of the night. The sergeant said the VC might have been trying to get on base to set some explosives. Nothing happened the rest of the night.

The next day everyone was asking me what had happened and if I was scared.

I said: "Hell yes I was scared, but what was I supposed to do? Let the VC get on the base?"

After chow, I came back to my hooch, and Lynn was sitting on my cot looking at my picture album of the photographs of my parents and siblings, but mostly she was looking at the houses. When I went to chow, I had forgotten to lock up the album. I always lock up everything when I left because things would seem to disappear. When I first walked in, she was surprised and frightened because she thought I would be mad at her for looking at my personal items. I sat down beside her, and she said she was sorry. I told her not to worry about it. It was hard for us to understand each other. She spoke very little English and I spoke even less Vietnamese. Lynn pointed her finger at me standing in front of my mother's house and asked if it was my home. She was amazed at how big it was. It really was not that big of a house, but to her it seemed big when you compared it to the average Vietnamese one-room houses or shacks. She asked if all GIs lived in big houses. She saw my '55 Chevy and asked if everyone had big cars. She asked me if I'd still be in the Army when I go home. She said one day that she hopes there would be no more war in Vietnam. She asked me if she could take my album home with her to show her family. I had to go with her at the end of her shift to the main gate to tell the MP it was all right for her to leave with the album because all Vietnamese were checked before leaving the compound.

The next morning my album was lying on my cot when I returned from chow. As I was about to leave the hooch, Lynn came up and thanked me for letting her take the album home. She had a few tears in her eyes as she turned to leave.

About a mile outside of our compound was an orphanage. There were about fifty orphans there whose parents were dead from either the war or something else. The week before Christmas, our company took a big box of toys, clothes, candy, and medicine to the orphanage. The kids were of all ages, and they were very happy to see us. There were a few that were half-Vietnamese and half-American. I felt very sorry and sad for the children when we were about to leave. A girl about ten years old came over to me and asked if I would come back and see them again. She said thank you for her doll and then, with tears in her eyes, she gave me a big hug. We did return occasionally when the opportunity was there, but not as often as I would have liked to.

CHAPTER 25

January 1970

One minute past midnight on January first, drunken soldiers were shooting off flares, M-14s, and M-16s, and it was like being in the middle of a full-scale firefight—or at least what I imagined it to be. Everyone was tense for a moment because no one had spent a previous New Year's Eve there, and for all anyone knew, we could have been under attack. It would have been a good time for one. It made everyone tense as Tet, the Vietnamese New Year, was just a few weeks away. The prior year, the enemy had launched an all-out devastating attack all over Vietnam on Tet. It was rumored that we were due again at any time. It was also rumored that on January second, those soldiers who had fired their guns had been demoted to a lower rank. The stupid soldiers who were firing should have known better, being in a war zone and all. For the whole month of January we had no convoys going off base. The last week of January, the base was put on alert because of the Vietnamese New Year. No one was allowed to go off base for any reason. Tet of 1970 in Nha Trang came and went with no attack from the enemy.

One night, Moose and I, along with another guy from our hooch who had just arrived in Vietnam, went to the NCO Club for some beer and listened to a band play. We had been there for about an hour when two of the Air Force guys that took our sandbags came into the club. They drank a beer and headed for the door to leave. As they passed our table, one of them was laughing and said they really liked the sandbags we filled for them. As they walked through the door, Moose was right behind them. Tim, the guy with us, asked what was going on, so I told him about how those guys took our sandbags from the beach that day.

He asked if Moose needed any help and I said, "No, there's only two of them."

We went outside and Moose had both of them in a headlock. He let one go and then kicked him in the ass and then let the other go and kicked him in the ass, too. The guys took off running, so we went back into the club for a few more beers. About a half-hour later, the two Air Force guys came into the club with five of their Air Force buddies. The two guys came over to Moose and said they were going to kick his ass.

Moose stood up and said: "You better go get some help. You're going to need more than seven of you."

So Moose grabbed the guy doing the talking and another guy and knocked their heads together and they fell unconscious. Tim picked up a beer bottle and hit a guy over the head with it. The guy was out like a light. Moose gave another guy an uppercut and he was down for the count. Tim got hit but came right back with a foot to the head on another guy, who went flying through the door to outside. I picked up a beer bottle and hit a guy across the nose and it started to bleed, but he stayed on his feet until Tim gave him another beer bottle to the back of the head. The last guy took off out the door. Moose had gotten three guys, Tim had gotten two and a half, I had gotten the other half, and the other ran away. About this time, the MPs showed up. The sergeant of the NCO Club told the MPs that the other guys had started the fight, but our first sergeant was called to the club anyway. When the first sergeant asked what was going on, we told him about the sandbags at the beach and what had happened. He told us to report to him in the morning at 9:00 am sharp.

The next morning at 9:00 am, the three of us reported to the first sergeant. He said if it were up to him, he would give the three of us a medal for taking care of seven guys from the Air Force. He did not like the Air Force for some reason. He said the CO got a call this morning from the Air Force CO and said he was mad as hell we had beat up his men, until he found out that only three of us took on his seven and won. The CO said to give us some easy punishment.

The first sergeant put us on shit-burning detail for the next three days. It may be an easy detail, but it sure was stinky. At least it only took half a day and then we were off for the last half of the day. Tim became a good friend of Moose and me. After burning the shit one day, Moose, Tim, and I went to the PX to get a few things. After leaving the PX, we ran into some of the Air Force guys from the fight we had at the NCO Club. They didn't say one word to us and walked on by.

When we got back to our hooch, we saw Lynn crying. We tried to ask her what she was crying about but it was hard to understand her Vietnamese. Moose left to get another hooch maid who spoke better English. The other hooch maid asked Lynn what was wrong, and she said that her five-year-old sister was very sick, and that her family was afraid she was going to die. The first sergeant was walking by and asked what was going on. After telling him, he said to take Lynn to her home and get the child and take her to the Base Hospital. He even said we could use his Jeep. Moose, Lynn, and I drove to her home, which was a very short distance off base, and took her sister and mother to the Base Hospital. The child was very sick and had a very high temperature. The doctor treated the child and said she would be all right in a few days. The doctor gave Lynn some medicine for the child and told her to give it to her until it was all gone.

We took Lynn and her mother back home, and when we arrived, about fifty or more people were waiting on us—Lynn's family and friends. Every one of them gave Moose and me a hug and kept saying, "Thank you," in Vietnamese. We found out the girl had an infection of some kind. Lynn lived with her mother, father, brother, and two sisters in a ten-by-twenty-foot hooch with no running water or electricity. This was common in Vietnamese homes. We had to leave and told Lynn to let us know if her family needed anything in the future. She was so thankful and she gave both of us a big hug and a kiss on the cheek. The next morning Lynn said her sister was much better and had no fever.

CHAPTER 26

February 1970

The second week of February, Moose, Tim, another soldier, and I went to Cam Ranh Bay on a two-truck convoy with MP escorts. We were going to pick up some supplies for our supply sergeant and ten Fucking New Guys (FNGs) who just came in-country. Moose was the driver going there and I was riding shotgun. Tim was driving the second truck. It was a very hot day, even at 8:00 am. By the time we arrived at Cam Ranh Bay, we were sweating like it had been raining on us. We got our supplies for the supply sergeant and then went to the 22nd Replacement Battalion to pick up the new guys. We were told it would be at least an hour before they would be ready to leave. So, you guessed it, we were off to the NCO Club for some beers. The MPs went to the MP Company to visit some friends, and we left our new guy who was riding with Tim behind to keep an eye on the trucks and Jeeps. Even on a military base with so many Vietnamese coming and going, you had to be careful. It was nice and cool inside the NCO Club. After Tim and I drank two beers apiece and Moose drank four, it was time to get back to the trucks. Moose could drink more beers than anybody I knew, except for maybe Carl.

We arrived back at our trucks and the MPs got there at the same time. The new guy was nowhere to be found. We checked over the trucks to make sure everything was still intact and see if anything was missing.

The new guy came walking up and said, "What's up?"

Moose was so mad that he had left the trucks and Jeeps unguarded you could almost see fire in his eyes. Moose told the guy to stand at attention. When you are called to attention, you stand with your feet and hands together with your eyes looking or staring straight forward and your arms hanging to your side. Moose began to chew the guy out, up one side and down the other. Moose was so mad because he had given the guy an order to stay with the trucks and, most of all, because the VC could recruit young Vietnamese children to place grenades in or on unattended trucks. It had happened before. A group of children had placed masking tape and rubber bands around the handle of a grenade, pulled the pin, and put the grenade down the fill pipe of a gas tank on a truck. In time, the gasoline or diesel fuel would release the hold of the tape or rubber band on the grenade and the truck would eventually explode. It happened about two weeks before around Saigon, killing two soldiers. We had just had a morning formation a few days back where they warned us not to leave any trucks unguarded at any time.

As Moose was chewing the guy out, the new FNGs had been watching from a short distance away. Moose told the guy to get in the truck because we were about to leave for Nha Trang. He went over to the ten new soldiers to check their orders and then told them to get in the back of the second truck. I had never seen men move so fast—they were nearly falling over each other getting up into the truck. Moose must have scared them pretty bad. Tim later told us that the guy was so scared and shaking that he didn't say a word the entire drive back.

After dropping off the new soldiers at the Replacement Company and getting the truck unloaded, we got cleaned up and went to chow. That was the first and last time I ever saw Moose so mad. As we were eating chow, I asked him if he was going to report Sam, the new guy, to the first sergeant for leaving the truck unattended. He said no, but he did ask Sam if he had learned a lesson. I asked Moose why Sam had left the trucks, and he said he was so mad that he forgot to ask him. Moose said now that he had calmed down he was going to ask Sam to go the NCO Club for a beer later. That was just the kind-hearted person Moose was. He would go out of his way to help you, but he was not a person you can walk over either. When Moose did ask Sam to go with us to the NCO Club, not a thing was said about what had happened at Cam Ranh Bay. We drank beer and listened to a band of Vietnamese trying to sing American rock 'n' roll. They were not very good at first, but by the time we left, they had gotten better. Maybe it was the beer we had consumed. On the way back to our hooch, Sam told Moose that he was sorry he had left the trucks unattended and that it would never happen again. Moose said not to worry about it because no one else knew anything about it, meaning he didn't tell the first sergeant. Tim and I couldn't walk a straight line back to the hooch, but Moose could and even helped the both of us back to our beds.

The next morning after chow, the first sergeant called Moose into the Orderly Room and said he had been put in for sergeant E-5. That evening, Moose, Tim, Sam, and I went downtown to Luc's Bar to celebrate.

As soon as we walked in, the bar girls came over to us and said: "No see you for long time. We make love with you?"

Some of the girls could speak a little English and some knew not a word. There were two girls each for the four of us. It only took two beers and a half-hour of the girls feeling up and down the leg of Tim and Sam before they left for a small room across the way. Mrs. Luc could speak the English language pretty well. She came over to Moose and me and asked if we had ever had a basket fuck. She said that a rope is looped through a pulley wheel attached to a beam over a bed. A girl sitting in a basket is then pulled up and over a GI lying on the bed. Two girls would position the basket over the GI and a third girl was gliding the basket over the GIs elevation after turning the girl in the basket around and around a dozen times and then letting go. Mrs. Luc talked us into it. I can only say that if you had never tried it, you don't know what you are missing. We left Luc's Bar and stumbled clumsily back to our company after having a very good night.

    The next morning my head was spinning out of control. I told myself I was never drinking again. We had shit-burning detail until midday, with the temperature around a hundred degrees. I was sweating so much. I guess it was mostly beer coming out, though. With the hangover, headache, heat, and smell, I was not having a very good day.

CHAPTER
27

March 1970

On March 2, 1970, I turned twenty-one years of age. The four of us, Moose, Tim, Sam and I, went to the NCO Club to celebrate my birthday and listened to a new Filipino band. One of their best songs was "Hey Jude" by the Beatles. They were one of the best bands we had heard so far. After leaving the club, we went back to our hooch and got some beer and went outside to sit on top of our bunker. Tim came out with a tape recorder. They were very popular at the time with all the soldiers in Vietnam. The tape players were small, battery operated, highly portable, and easy to carry. Tim put on the song by the Animals, "We Gotta Get Out of This Place." It was one of the most popular songs in Vietnam with the enlisted men. The next song was by Jimi Hendrix, "Purple Haze." That's when the marijuana was very easy to get, and most of the soldiers I knew were either smoking it or drinking beer. Or both. If you didn't smoke weed or drink beer when you first came to Vietnam, you definitely did by the time you left. As the next song began to play, "Light My Fire," by the Doors, the Air Force guys began firing their big guns at the mountain back behind the base. They fired round after round for a good ten to fifteen minutes, and then a half-dozen choppers began firing their tracer rounds into the mountain. With getting high on the marijuana and drunk on the beer, we had one heck of a show going on.

On the seventh of March, Moose went in front of the promotion board for sergeant E-5 with ten other soldiers. It would be two weeks before he would find out if he got it or not. Also on the same day, my six-month mark in Vietnam hit. After six months in Vietnam, a soldier could go on R&R to his choice of several places to spend five days away from the war. R&R stands for Rest and Recovery. Or Relaxation. Or Recuperation. Nobody ever really knows what the second R stands for. R&R is when you get to leave the war zone, and that's all that mattered to us. Moose and I had been talking about going to Bangkok, Thailand, together. Most married guys would go to Hawaii to meet their wives or girlfriends. I had a hard time deciding between the two because of the way things were between Paula and me. In one letter she said she would meet me there, then the next letter she said she wouldn't. I decided to put in for Hawaii, hoping Paula would be there. Moose left for Bangkok and I left for Hawaii on the third week of March.

I arrived at the airport in Hawaii around noon, and as the men were getting off the plane, their wives or girlfriends came running over to give them hugs and kisses. I looked all over for Paula, but she was nowhere to be found. I began to wish I had gone to Bangkok with Moose. I got a taxi to the hotel where I had made reservations. After I had checked in and gotten the room key, I went to the hotel bar and had two cold beers before going up to my room. As I was about to leave the bar, a very attractive and sexy girl, maybe in her late twenties, asked me to buy her a drink. So I did. She asked if I was stationed in Vietnam and currently on R&R.

I said, "Yes, my wife was supposed to meet me here but she wasn't at the airport when I got here."

She said that it happens all the time with the GIs. She asked if I would like to go up to her room with her for a good time. I said why not. First, I had to take my things up to my room and get cleaned up. She gave me her room number and left. As I was unlocking the door to my room, Paula came walking up. What a surprise. I asked her why she wasn't at the airport, and she said she was late getting there and came back to the hotel hoping I'd be there.

That first night we did a lot of talking about our marriage. I thought we may have worked things out, but the next day Paula began acting like she didn't know what she was going to do. One minute she said she loved me and the next minute she wasn't so sure. All things considered, I tried to have a good time with her and enjoy being in Hawaii and not in Vietnam. To tell the truth, the way Paula was acting, I was ready to get back to my friends in Vietnam. I had done my best to keep our marriage together—more than most men would have done. Or so I was told by more than one person. I had to accept the reality and move on. Our last day in Hawaii, I took Paula to catch her plane because she was leaving first. As she turned to get on her plane, she said that she hoped I would be all right and that she was sorry about everything. Only time would tell.

I arrived back in Vietnam with the temperature already hot at 8:00 am. As it turned out, Moose had just arrived from Bangkok and was getting into the back of the truck, too. As I walked up to the truck to get in, a new guy, an FNG, said there was no more room and to get on another truck.

Moose took the guy by the arm and said, "Get your very new ass off this truck before I throw you off."

The guy could not get off fast enough. Moose helped me get into the truck. After arriving at the 22nd Replacement Battalion, we found a hooch and a cot and locked our things in it and headed off to the NCO Club. After telling Moose about Paula and our time in Hawaii—and that I wished I had gone to Bangkok with him instead—he said that he was sorry it didn't work out for us. He got us another beer—his third and my second, but who's counting?

I asked him how his R&R went, and with a big smile on his face, he began to tell me everything. He said that finding girls proved to be no problem there. He didn't even have to go to a bar. Within minutes of closing the door behind him in his hotel room, there was a knock on the door.

A smiling Chinese man greeted him and said: "You won pretty girl to-ni? I have ni girl. You goo company to-ni. Okay?"

He said he didn't want a girl right then because he was too tired and hadn't showered and rested. The man talked him into allowing him to bring a girl up for an appraisal, though. He let them out and then took a shower. As Moose was shaving, he heard another knock on the door. It was the Chinese man again with another attractive girl. He said his resistance was melting fast, and within minutes he agreed to the company of the girl. Prostitution was sanctioned and regulated and the girls were regularly inspected by their governmental health authorities. For $25, a girl was yours for twenty-four hours. He said he dreamt about lying next to a pretty, soft thing all day and screwing every hour, but the next thing he knew, he drifted off until morning.

The next day, Moose and the Chinese girl went sightseeing. She took him all over Bangkok. He said it was a nice and clean city, filled with industrious people moving at a fast pace. They were used to GIs and didn't look twice when you walked down the street. They went to a peaceful city park filled with parents and their children. She took him to a Chinese bath house where girls washed you from head to toe. After that, he said he was ready to go back to the room for some love-making. By this time, his twenty-four hours were up so they said their goodbyes.

After the girl left, he said there was yet another knock on the door. It was the same Chinese man with two more young and attractive girls. He said he could have one for $25 or both for $40. He could have them all night until the next morning. Moose took the two for $40 and had one nice time.

CHAPTER 28

April 1970

After getting back to Nha Trang via helicopter, I was ready for a cold beer. The pilot of the chopper was new to Vietnam and was ready for some action. Instead of flying along the coastline where it was safer, he flew inland over the jungle. Moose and I just looked at each other—*What the fuck is this pilot doing?* About halfway to Nha Trang, we began to take on sniper fire. You could hear the rounds hit the chopper. The door gunners opened up with their M-60s, and the look on the pilot's face said it all: "I fucked up." After getting off the chopper at Nha Trang, we walked around the chopper and counted ten holes where we had been hit. If Moose could have gotten ahold of the pilot, I think he would've killed him. The pilot just sat in the chopper until we were gone.

At morning formation the next day (which was seldom lately), the first sergeant called for Moose to come forward. He got his promotion to sergeant E-5: three stripes, and about $70 more pay each month. I was very happy for him, and I knew he would make a fine sergeant. At the same time, I was a little sad because I knew I would have to ride with another soldier on my convoys because E-5s or higher rarely had to go on convoys.

That night, Moose, Tim, Sam, and I went downtown to Luc's Bar to celebrate. Mrs. Luc was glad to see us.

As we sat down, the girls came over and hit us with, "You buy me Saigon Tea?"

We had been drinking for some time when about half a dozen Vietnamese soldiers came into the bar. After a few beers, one of them came over to our table and said something in Vietnamese. He went back to his table and pointed his finger at us and began to laugh with his friends. He then came back over and began talking in Vietnamese again.

We asked Mrs. Luc what he was saying, and with a fearful look on her face she said, "He thinks he can whip the big one with the sergeant stripes by himself in only five minutes or less."

With a look of surprise on his face, he turned and left and then came back with the other five guys.

Tim, Sam, and I asked Moose if we should leave and he said, "No, there's only six of them."

Moose had gotten up by this time, and as the men came over, he gave one of his round-house kicks and took out two of them, and then with another kick, he took out two more. He then gave an uppercut to the other two guys. It couldn't have taken any more than two minutes. We didn't even have time to get up and help him. Moose gave no man any shit, but he also didn't take any from anybody either, no matter who they were. Mrs. Luc came over and asked us to leave before more Vietnamese soldiers came because she didn't want any more trouble. We left and stopped at the NCO Club for some more beers.

Moose had a very kind and gentle personality, but he was not the type of guy who would ever back down to anyone. Tim, Sam, and I were just amazed at how easily Moose made things look. We left the NCO Club and went back to our hooch a little early because the next day was full of activity for our new sergeant. We also had to get things ready for a ten-truck convoy to another Army unit about twenty miles northwest of us. We were delivering building material, a lot of water, food, and ammunition because the unit was a new outpost on some mountain.

The morning of our convoy, Moose came to see us off. He was telling me what to do and what to watch out for. He told the new guy who was riding shotgun with me to pay attention and we would be all right. This was the new guy's first convoy. He had only been in-country for ten days. We left at 7:30 am and it took us three hours to get there. We drove through the jungle on some of the worst roads I have ever driven on. We could only go about twenty or twenty-five miles per hour. It was a hot day, too. The new guy did all right, but he sure was a talker. I missed Moose because most of the time he only spoke if he really had something interesting to say or something that might get your interest up. I could tell it would not be the same without him.

By the time all the trucks were unloaded, it was too late to start back because it was going to be getting dark soon. We spent the night on the mountaintop with the infantry guys, and it made me thankful I was a truck driver and not one of them. I could not envision spending my tour of duty as an infantryman in Vietnam, staying out in the jungle for an entire year. All through the night we would hear the sound of small-arms fire in the near distance. We all expected to be attacked at any time. None of us got much sleep that night. We took turns trying to sleep, but it was no use. Nothing happened during that night, thankfully. At first light, we headed back to Nha Trang, and I was so glad to get back. The first thing I did, after putting away my gear, was head for the showers to wash off all the dust, dirt, and grime. We all were so dirty from the sweat. I stayed in the shower for an hour.

Noon came and it was time for chow. When I got to the Mess Hall, Moose was already there.

I walked over to him and said, "Sergeant, is this spot taken?"

He looked up and said with a big smile on his face, "Sit your ass down, Specialist Lott."

He then asked how the convoy went and how the new guy did. I told him everything went fine but if I had to go on another convoy with him, I was going to put some tape over his mouth. About this time, the new guy come over and sat down next to us and began talking some more. Ten minutes later, he was still talking and had not taken one bite of food. As Moose and I got up to leave, the guy just turned to another soldier and kept on talking. Moose said he was glad the guy was in another hooch because if he weren't, then he would be soon. Moose said all he did on his first day of being sergeant was supervise some guys on filling sandbags and shit-burning.

I went to the PX to get a few things, and as I was leaving, one of the Army cars pulled up and a lieutenant colonel got out and went into the PX. The driver stayed in the car, so I walked over and asked him how long he had been driving his car. He said he'd been driving for eight months. We got to talking and found out we both got in-country on the same day. I asked him what his duty was besides being a driver for an officer. He said on normal days he would arrive at the Billet Quarters for Officers at 6:00 am and take the colonel to morning chow and then take him to his office. At noon, he would take him back to the Mess Hall and then back to his office. He would pick him up around 6:00 pm from his office and take him back to his quarters—then do it all over again the next day. He said it was a little boring but that it was much better than being in the infantry. He said about two times a week he would drive him to the PX or the beach for a swim. He said that it was a nice job to have. I asked him if he ever got to leave base, and he said he'd only been to downtown Nha Trang one time.

He asked what I did, and I told him about truck driving for the 10th Logistical Support Group South. He said he'd heard of us and all the convoys we got to go on. He said he would hate to do that for a year and then asked how often we got shot at. About then, the colonel came walking up so I gave him a salute and headed back to the hooch.

Back at the hooch, I found out I had guard duty that night. The guy who was supposed to have it had a very bad case of diarrhea. He had been to downtown Nha Trang the night before and caught something from the Vietnamese food. We had all been warned not to eat their food or drink their water. The Vietnamese lack of sanitation and the filth led to infectious conditions. So I took his guard duty knowing I would have the next day off.

I reported for guard duty and Moose was on duty as sergeant of the guard. He would take each of six men to guard posts and then every hour come around to check on us. After taking the other men to their posts, Moose dropped me off at the guard tower. The structure was twenty-five feet high with a ladder to climb to the top. At the top of the tower, you had a clear view all around the perimeter of the razor-sharp barbed wire that separated the jungle from the base. This was my first time at that particular tower. I had guard duty from 9:00 pm till midnight.

Everything was quiet, free from any noise since the tower was secluded from the other guard posts and the main part of the base. After about hour two of my three-hour duty, a funny thing happened. Of course it wasn't funny at the time, though. The night was very still with no noise up until that point. It was so peaceful I almost fell asleep. I didn't, however, because you do not sleep while on guard duty or you could be court-martialed.

To my right on the other side of the barbed wire, I hear a "Fuck you."

A few minutes later I heard another: "Fuck you."

I began to worry a little. I grabbed my M-16 rifle, put it on full automatic, and took the safety off. I was thinking I was about to be attacked by the VC.

Off to my left was another: "Fuck you."

Then another and another. By this time, I was getting pissed off. The area outside the barbed wire was a free-fire zone, and I was getting so mad I was about to fire at the sound. Just as I raised up the M-16 to fire, Moose came driving up. He climbed up the tower and could tell I was a little pissed-off. I told him what was going on, and he began laughing. I had never seen him laugh so hard. He had tears in his eyes. I didn't think it was funny, so I was beginning to get mad at him. He finally stopped laughing enough to tell me why he was laughing.

He said, "I thought you knew about the lizard."

I said, "What does a lizard have to do with you laughing so hard?"

He said, "The lizard is a gecko, and the sound they make is a 'fuck you' sound."

They sound just like a person, and it can be hard to tell them apart. Moose said that I wouldn't have been the first soldier to shoot at one. As we climbed down the ladder, there was another "fuck you," and I thought Moose was going to fall off the ladder he was laughing so hard.

As my replacement was climbing up the ladder, Moose said in a low voice, "Beware of the lizard."

The last week of April is very hard for me to write about, but a time I think about almost every day since leaving Vietnam. The day was very hot, like any other day. We had not had a convoy for a few weeks, so we were either pulling shit-burning detail or my least favorite, guard duty, or filling sandbags. On this day, Tim, Sam, a few other soldiers, and I were on a painting detail. We had to give anything that was green a new coat of paint. Everything in the Army is olive-drab green. It was almost noon, and we all were soaked with sweat. Moose, who was in charge of the detail, had been sitting in the shade.

Every now and then he would say to Sam, Tim, or me, "You missed a spot. Don't make me look bad," then he would laugh.

Moose left to go to the latrine to take a piss, and while he was gone, Tim, Sam, and a few others took some empty paint cans and filled them with water and put the lids back on them. Moose came back and sat down and began to tell us what a messy job we were doing, a big smile on his face. We all looked at each other and then took the lids off the paint cans and told him we had all we were going to take from him. As we picked up the cans and walked his way, he had this funny look on his face.

He said, "Wait a minute."

But before he could say another word, we threw the water on him. He was so surprised because he was certain paint was in the cans.

A big smile came on his face and he said, "Okay, detail is over for the day."

After taking a shower and going to chow, we were off to the NCO Club for a cold beer. The first round was on Moose. After a few beers it was time for Tim and Sam to leave because they had guard duty later. With nothing else to do, Moose and I went downtown to Luc's Bar. It was just starting to get dark as we arrived. I never did like going to Luc's at night because it was very uncomfortable walking down the dark streets. I was always expecting to get shot at or be taken prisoner by the VC. We were always reminded about the VC coming out at night. This night for some reason, I just had a bad feeling that something was not right. I told Moose how I was feeling, and he said we would only have a couple of beers and then head back. Normally there are people coming and going and kids playing in the streets, but on this night there were hardly any Vietnamese out and about. There were no noises except for a dog barking in the distance.

As we entered the bar, it was very quiet with no activity. There were no bar girls. Only Mrs. Luc was there. She was not her normal happy self, either. We asked her where all the girls were, and she said that none of them came to work tonight. As Mrs. Luc sat our beers on the table, she said in a low voice, "You guys should leave, it isn't safe tonight."

I told Moose we should leave and he said, "After one more beer."

I had to piss, so I got up and walked to the back of the bar and out the back door because there was no modern plumbing inside. As I was about to step back inside the bar, I saw Moose leaning from his chair with his arm extending out like he was trying to reach for something.

Then I heard Moose yell, "Grenade!"

The next thing I knew, I was lying on my back. As I tried to get up, my head was pounding and my ears ringing. I could hardly see with all the dust in the air. Then I remembered that Moose yelled "grenade."

Now I knew what Moose was trying to reach for. All of a sudden I was filled with fear of going back into the bar, afraid of finding Moose dead. As I entered, I could see Mrs. Luc lying behind the bar with no sign of being hurt. She was just shaken up and frightened.

As the dust and smoke settled, I could see Moose lying on the floor. I ran over to him and I could tell he was hurt badly. Mrs. Luc came over with a small towel and began wiping the blood from his face. She was crying and said a grenade was tossed through the door and Moose had tried to reach for it. My guess was he was trying to throw it back out the door as it exploded. I was trying to talk to him when he opened his eyes and asked if I was all right. Then he closed his eyes and his head rolled away and I knew he was gone.

Just then, MPs came running in and I said we needed to get him to the Base Hospital. We carried him to the Jeep, and in less than five minutes we were at the hospital. It didn't matter, though. Moose was gone. I just couldn't believe Moose was dead. It all seemed like a bad dream. One minute we were drinking beer, laughing, and having a good time. I kept thinking if I had not gotten up to go take a piss when I did, then I might have been able to throw the grenade back out the door instead of him. Or I might be the one lying dead in the hospital.

Now I had lost two of my best friends in this war—first Bob, now Moose. I think of them both and wonder how it would have been without this damn war. As I was sitting outside the hospital trying to think of how I was going to tell Tim and Sam, the first sergeant drove up and asked me to tell him what had happened. He knew that we were best friends, and he began telling me how over the years in the Army, he had lost some good friends, too. He said I could have the next day off to get my head straight. After the sergeant left, I walked over to the NCO Club and drank a few more beers, trying to remember just how everything had happened—and if I could have done anything to prevent it. After I decided that there was not a thing I could have done, I walked back to the hospital to say my goodbyes to Moose.

After returning to the hooch, I lay down on my cot but couldn't sleep. Later that night, Tim and Sam returned from guard duty. They came over to me and asked why I was still up and where Moose was. They had heard that some GI was seriously hurt downtown but they didn't know who it was.

Then they both said at the same time, "Was it Moose?"

All I could do was nod my head up and down. Before they could say anything, I said that he was dead. They asked what had happened. After I told them, they sat there in disbelief. Tim had tears in his eyes and Sam kept saying that it couldn't be true and kept walking back and forth. We stayed up the rest of the night talking, drinking beer, and telling funny things about each other.

The next morning, we had one of those rare morning formations. The first sergeant called me to the front and asked if I would or could explain to everyone what had happened the night before. I got halfway through it but couldn't go any further. Everyone was in disbelief. For the next week, I did a lot of thinking about Moose, wondering if I could stand being in this company anymore, remembering him every time I walked into our hooch and lay down by his empty cot. I decided to put in a transfer to the Transportation Company across the base from us, next to the Air Force base. After telling Tim and Sam what I had done, we all three went to the NCO Club to say our goodbyes over a few beers.

CHAPTER
29

May 1970

The second week of May, I was called into the first sergeant's office. He gave me my transfer orders for the 297th Transportation Company and asked me if I had changed my mind. He said he understood my reason for leaving and wished me luck. He said I was to report to my new company anytime tomorrow. I went back to my hooch and began packing my gear. The new guy walked in and asked me where he should put his gear. He asked if the cot next to mine was empty. I told him it was, and then he asked if the person had gone home.

I said: "Yes he did. The war is over for him."

After getting everything packed and ready to go, I walked over to the NCO Club to be alone and to think. I was thinking how lucky I had been over the last eight months since arriving in Vietnam and how lucky I was to have friends like Sam and Tim. Also, how lucky I was to have known a person like Moose.

It was getting late so I headed back to the company. As I was walking beside the road, a car pulled up beside me. It was the same guy I had talked to at the PX. He asked if I would like a ride. I obliged and got in. He asked how I was getting along and if I had been on any convoys lately. He asked if I knew the guy who was killed downtown a few weeks back. I told him all about what had happened at the bar that night and that I had asked for a transfer to his company. I told him I would be reporting there sometime tomorrow.

After he dropped me off at my hooch, he said, "I'll see you tomorrow."

That night, Tim and Sam gave me a going-away party, even though I was only going across the base. We were all outside sitting on our bunker, drinking beer, and Tim came out with his tape recorder to put some music on. We were all having a good time until the alert siren went off. We all went for our M-16 rifles, but as soon as we got to our duty station, the all-clear whistle went off. So we returned to the party. We drank and smoked some weed and told stories to each other. Tim said that after he got out of the Army he would buy his own big-rig truck and travel all around the country. Sam said that he had been thinking about making a career out of the Army, and if that didn't work out then he didn't know what he was going to do. I told them I didn't know yet, but the way I was feeling right then, I would not be staying in the Army. That night was the last time the three of us were together as a group. Sam ended up going home on an emergency leave the following week. I never had a chance to say goodbye because, after being notified of his family's medical problem, Sam was taken to the airport and was on his way home within two hours. He never came back to Vietnam either. Why? We never found out.

The next morning after coming back from chow, I gathered up my gear and went to the first sergeant's office to say my goodbyes. The sergeant had a company clerk drive me over to my new company in his Jeep. I arrived there around mid-morning, and no one was there except for an E-4 company clerk by the name of Miller. He said I could find a cot in one of the hooches of my choice. E-4 Miller seemed to be something of a dumbass. He said he had no idea where or when the first sergeant would be back. I walked in and out of a half-dozen hooches until I ran into the guy who had given me a ride the night before. I said I was looking for an empty cot to put my gear.

He said, "How about this one next to mine?"

His name was E-4 Carson, and he was from New York.

After getting my gear put away, it was time for chow, so Carson and I walked over to the Mess Hall. On our way back to our hooch, we walked by the Fifth Special Forces Operations Base that was across the road and just behind my hooch. On this day, about twenty or so Special Forces soldiers were standing in formation when an Army sedan pulled up and a three-star general got out. It was some sort of ceremony, and he was giving out medals to the men. I didn't know it then, but I would be seeing that general every day before too long. He gave out a few Army Commendation Medals, Bronze Stars, and Purple Hearts. I was thinking to myself, *I sure hope I never receive a Purple Heart.*

Carson and I watched for a while and then went back toward our hooch. As we were about to enter, the first sergeant came walking up and asked if I was the new guy who had just transferred to his company. I said I was, and then he told me that I would be riding with Carson for the next two days to get to know how my job would be. Carson said this is one of the best jobs in the Army if you can put up with some of the dumbass officers. He said some of them could be a real pain in the ass, but there were also some that were all right to be around. He said that it would not take very long to tell the difference. Carson was a bright guy, and we got along pretty well.

The next morning, we went to the motor pool to check out the car we would be driving for the day. Each day you would or wouldn't be driving the same car. At the end of the day, you returned the car to the motor pool and did it all over again the next day. We would get to the motor pool by 6:00 am every morning and then to the officer's billet or officer's quarters by 6:15 am. Some drivers were assigned to a certain officer. If not, then whoever was the first officer to get to your car would be your assignment that day. I never did understand why more than one officer would not ride in the same car. It seemed that each officer had to have his own ride.

We would take them to morning chow and then to the "Grand Hotel," a four-story building built by the French. Sitting in the middle of the compound, it was now the Headquarters and Command Center of "First Field Force Vietnam" in the two-corps area of Vietnam. Vietnam was divided into four corps—one corps in the north, two corps in the middle of the country where I was stationed, and one corps in the south. After dropping the officer off at the Command Center, we would return to the officer's billet to pick up another officer and then go back to the Command Center. If two or three officers had ridden in the same car together, it would have been a lot easier and would have made a lot more sense. But this was the Army, and what did a lowly enlistee like me know?

On most days after getting the officers to their work areas, we were free to do as we pleased until it was time to pick them up and take them back to their quarters. Some days we would go to the PX and get things we were short of or go to the beach for a few hours or go back to our hooch and catch up on some sleep. This duty is what I would call a REMF paradise, a term used by front-line soldiers to describe those in cushy jobs in the rear, even though in Vietnam, there really was no front line or rear. There were some places that were safer than others, but the whole country was still a war zone. You could get killed at any time or in any place. Snipers, incoming rockets—even sitting in a bar downtown could get you killed.

I stayed in a hooch with a bunch of potheads, and like most nights, they would put on some rock 'n' roll music and get high on songs by the Animals, Jimi Hendrix, and the Doors. "Purple Haze" by Jimi Hendrix was the most popular song to get high on. There was never too much said by the first sergeant about guys smoking pot as long as they smoked it on their off-duty time and didn't cause trouble. Even the first sergeant would come by from time to time and smoke a little with us. The first sergeant was a lifer, someone that made a career out of the Army, but he was also a nice lifer. He took care of his men and understood what his men had to put up with on a daily basis because he had been one of us at some point in his career. He would come by our hooch occasionally just to talk one on one and have a beer. If there was a problem, he would try and solve it for the soldiers.

My first night, he came into my hooch and, as I was sitting on my cot writing a letter, he asked me how my first day had gone and if I thought I would like it here after going on convoys through the jungle and getting shot at. He had been in the

Army for twenty-three years and planned to stay for another seven and retire at the age of forty-eight. At the time, I was only twenty-one, but forty-eight seemed pretty old to me. He was from a small town in southwestern Oklahoma. Since we were both Okies, we had something in common we could talk about and share together.

Whenever we met each other around the company area, he would say, "How are you doing today, Okie?"

I would always say, "Just fine, Okie," if no one else was around.

If there were other soldiers around, I would call him first sergeant.

Normally, when you pull up to the Officer's Quarters, they would be waiting and just get inside the car. But about three weeks into my driving, I pulled up and a lieutenant colonel I had never seen before was just standing there, and I couldn't figure out why he was not getting into the car. After about a minute or so, he opened the door and got inside.

The first thing that he said: "Driver, do you not understand the procedure for opening a door for an officer? Next time, I expect you to open my door for me."

I said, "Yes, sir."

However, in my head I was thinking, *What a lifer and a dumbass.*

That night back in the hooch, I told Carson about the colonel and what he said to me, and Carson said he had heard about the guy. He said there was nothing we could do about it because the colonel was right about the procedure. About a week later as I pulled up to the Officer's Quarters, the same colonel was waiting on a ride, and I was thinking to myself, *Not again.*

I pulled up and got out to open the door for him, but before I could get around the car, he had opened it and gotten in. I got back into the car and he said: "Good morning, driver. How's your day going so far?"

From that day on, he was always nice, courteous, and polite to me. He turned out not to be a dumbass after all. Well, maybe a little bit.

I was called into the first sergeant's office, and he said that the next day there would be two Very Important Persons (VIPs) arriving at the airport, and that I was assigned to pick them up and take them to the First Field Force Headquarters and serve as their driver for the rest of the day. The VIPs were two senators. I arrived at the airport as a lieutenant general was arriving with his MP convoy of two Jeeps with M-60 machine guns mounted behind the driver of each Jeep. After the general had greeted the senators, we pulled out of the airbase and turned right onto Beach Road and headed south for about three miles. We came to a Vietnamese Compound where a meeting with some high-ranking Vietnamese generals was taking place. After two hours, we left the compound and drove back to the First Field Force Headquarters. After another two hours, we left and drove back to the air base, where the two senators got on their small jet and headed to another base somewhere north of Nha Trang. It was the first of many VIPs I would drive for.

On one occasion, I went to the airbase to pick up another senator, a congressman, and Four-Star General Westmoreland, who was commander of the U.S. forces in Vietnam. We left the airbase and headed for the First Field Force Headquarters with more MPs than I had ever seen before. They were all along the route we were taking, with every Jeep carrying an M-60 and gunships flying overhead. After all, there was a senator, congressman, the commanding general of First Field Force, and the commander of all U.S. forces in Vietnam—and my lowly specialist E-4 self. The VC would have loved to have taken these people out. As we turned left onto Beach Road, I looked in the rearview mirror and I could see two Vietnamese men on a motorbike. They were trying the pass the MP Jeeps behind us. On the last try, the MP Jeep pulled over to the side of the motorbike and ran it off the road into a ditch. If the motorbike had gotten past the MPs and up to the cars we were driving, someone would had gotten into a lot of trouble because the job of the MPs was to keep all vehicles behind the convoy no matter who they were. The motorbike could have pulled up beside the general's car and tossed a grenade in it.

We turned left off Beach Road and into the headquarters compound and pulled up in front of the Grand Hotel. As I stopped the car, a colonel there opened the rear door for General Westmoreland but did not give the general a salute.

After getting out of the car, General Westmoreland leaned over to the colonel and asked in a low voice, "Don't you give a salute to a superior officer?"

The colonel said, "Yes, sir," as he snapped to attention and gave a salute with a very red face.

General Westmoreland then reached out his hand and they both shook and walked into the headquarters building.

We were told the meeting would last about four hours, so I decided to walk the short distance to the NCO Club for a beer and get something to eat. We were not supposed to drink beer while on duty, but I figured one beer would wear off in four hours. Besides, I was young and sometimes I didn't think things through. Three beers later, someone came into the club asking if the driver for General Westmoreland was there. He said that the meeting was over and that I should get back to the car and be ready to leave. The meeting was over in less than an hour. I left the club and got back to my car just as the VIPs and the general came walking out of the building. I always kept some candy mints in the car, so I reached in and got a handful and put them in my mouth, hoping no one would smell the odor of beer on me. If they did, I could be in for some real trouble, like getting a court-martial. Luckily, no one smelled beer and we left for the airbase.

After everyone had gotten on the small jet plane, I was off duty so I got some chow and then went back to the NCO Club for a cold beer. What a day. I was only going to have one or two beers, but there was supposed to be a new band playing so I stayed and had more beers than I had planned on. The band never did show up, so I decided to go back to my hooch and get some sleep. After I staggered back to the hooch, I remember trying to get the mosquito-net apparatus set up. I draped the net and tucked it in the end under the mattress. I crawled into the little enclosure and laid down and fell into a drunken stupor, not seeing the abundance of inch-round holes in my mosquito net that would not keep little sparrows out. I woke up the next morning with a head-splitting, throbbing hangover. In addition, I was covered with hundreds of mosquito bites. My skin was puffed and hardened and itched all over. There were more mosquitos inside my net than in all the rest of Vietnam. It took me a few minutes to realize where I was. I did not have to go to work that day because it was Sunday. What a lifesaver. I did not function much that morning.

During the morning, I laid around trying to recuperate, mourning my condition. I thought about home only marginally now. There was too much going on and too many new things with my job to think about it. During the day, the mosquitoes weren't as bad. I went to the Supply Building and got a new net. After the prior night's experience, I carefully inspected the new net and made sure it was strategically tucked in all around my cot. How all those holes got into my old net, I don't know.

The last week of May, I put in for a three-day pass. I really didn't think I would get one, but I went ahead and put in anyway. To my surprise, it went through. I slept in late each morning, went to chow, and went to the beach every day. After three days on the beach, I was beginning to get a nice suntan. With nine months down and three more to go, I was getting short.

CHAPTER 30

June 1970

There was an important ritual performed daily by the troops who spent a tour in Vietnam, excluding the lifers. It was as important as daily mass to a priest. It actually had to do with a devotional rite to one of the few things that added up: time. Each morning before we did anything else, we pulled out a varying number of calendars to mark off another day gone. Another day closer to going home and leaving the war to the next guy. The variety of calendars, free-hand drawings, and commercial printings were what was known as "short-timers' calendars." The term was probably a misnomer that everyone was short, as many of the counters were started within a month of arriving in-country. They all had a primary direction, though, in bringing an owner to that state of shortness: hence the label. The differences in men were reflected in their portfolio of calendars. Some men had more than one, ranging from simple pages of straight months and days to gross caricatures containing blocked-off divisions of descending numbers. One of these latter representations was the kind I had.

It was a perfectly proportioned Amazon woman standing nude and spread-eagled the length of the page. Beneath her and between her legs stood a midget GI with his head upturned and his disproportionately long tongue flicking out at her genitals with a wild, happy, excited look in his eyes. The midget, of course, was "short," and the area of his interest was triangularly blocked off and contained the last number—the number one, signifying the last day in-country. When a soldier got to one hundred days left on his tour of duty in Vietnam, he was considered to be a short-timer. As of the first week of June 1970, I had ninety-four days left. I was getting short.

That first week of June, I was called into the first sergeant's office. He asked how things were going and if I liked the job of driving for the VIPs. He said he had gotten a lot of good reports on me, that I was doing an excellent job. He said that the following week, the driver for Lieutenant General Collins would be on R&R and that I would be taking his place, driving for the general. I was to report to the general's villa, his living quarters, on Monday at 6:30 am.

The villa, built by the French when they fought the Vietnamese, was a three-story brick building with living quarters in the back for servants. The villa was a mile north of the Headquarters and Command Center. The villa sat on about an acre of land with guard posts manned by both American and Vietnamese MPs. It was a very well-secured area. Also living in the villa on the compound was a brigadier general, a major general, and an assortment of personnel to do the cooking, cleaning, laundry, and driving. A cook or chef was on twenty-four-hour duty to prepare the greatest of food fare—lobster, prime rib, steaks, or anything whatsoever on short notice at any time of day or night for the generals. What a life in a war zone. The 272nd MP Company was stationed about a block down the street from the villas. Every day, everywhere the general went, we would have an escort accompanying us. I got to know a lot of the MPs and became friends with them.

That next Monday morning, just past 6:00 am, I arrived at the villa. I didn't want to be late so I got there a little early just to be sure where to park my car. It would not have been good to keep a general waiting. After backing the car up into the driveway, I got out and walked around to the back door on the right side and opened it to make sure it was clean for the general. About this time, a Jeep pulled up with two MPs, so I went over and said I would be driving for the general this week while his driver was on R&R. I knew one of them from driving the VIPs around. As I went back to the car, a captain came out of the villa and said good morning to me and asked how long I had been in Vietnam. He asked where I was from in the States and if I liked driving for VIPs and generals. He was a very nice person. Not ordinary for a captain's status. Another captain came out and never said a word to me. He was not very nice. He was the kind of officer who thought he was better than the lowly enlisted personnel. The first captain, Captain Morse, and I got along just fine. I could talk to him about everything. We did just that, too. He was a funny guy. He was always telling me a joke to make me laugh. The other, Captain Dumbass, as I would call him behind his back (naturally), we never got along. The two captains were the general's aides-de-camp. Their duties and responsibilities were to personally assist the general with any and all jobs, anything that would help the general do his job.

At 7:00 am sharp, General Collins came out of the villa. He walked over to where I was standing beside the open car door. I was standing at attention and I gave him a salute.

He returned my salute and said, "Good morning, driver," and got into the car.

My fear at that moment was shutting the car door on his foot before he got it into the car. We pulled out of the villa with the two MPs in their Jeeps following close behind. We turned right going east until we came to Beach Road. It was already hot and there were a lot of Vietnamese walking alongside the road. There were soldiers sitting on the beach drinking what appeared to be beers. If not for the war, you would have thought this was the perfect vacation place to be with your wife or girlfriend. About a mile up on Beach Road, we turned right again into the Headquarters and Command Center Compound with both American and Vietnamese MPs at the guard posts. I pulled up in front of the Headquarters Building, where the two captains and the general got out and went into the building.

I found a place to park and sat and observed what was going on inside the compound. There were old Vietnamese men and women doing various things like sweeping the front of the building and picking up trash. More cars pulled up with more officers, and then the drivers would try to find a place to park as close to the building as possible so they could see when their officers were coming out. I took a walk around the compound to check the place out.

Back behind the Headquarters Building was a Mess Hall. Also behind and to the right were some hooches for new guys waiting for orders to their duty stations. These were the same hooches I stayed in back in September when I was waiting for my orders. On the other side of the compound was a barbershop run by the Vietnamese. About two months later, the Vietnamese barber was found to be a VC. There was also an NCO Club and an EM Club.

I had to take a piss, so I walked up the steps to go inside the Headquarters Building and was stopped by a MP asking who I was and where I was going. This was one big man and one MP I had not seen before. After telling him I was a driver for General Collins, he let me go inside. Being the driver for a three-star general had its rewards, as I would find out later. The building had the first inside latrine I had seen since being in Vietnam.

After leaving the latrine, I decided to take a tour of the place and found where the general's office was. I found the office on the second floor. The door was open so I walked in and a specialist E-7 was sitting behind a desk doing some typing.

He took a look at my nametag and said: "You must be Specialist Lott. I've heard a lot of good things about you."

We talked for a while, and I could tell he was a nice guy I could get along well with. He said he was going to give me a walkie-talkie so he could call me when the general was leaving the building so I could have the car in front waiting for him. He said I was to have the walkie-talkie with me at all times and not to let it out of my sight. That walkie-talkie came in handy more than a few times.

Around this time, Captain Dumbass came in and interrupted Specialist Fox and me without excusing himself.

He looked at me and said, "Don't you have something to do, Private Lott?"

I said: "Yes, I do sir. But I am not a private, I am a specialist, sir."

After Captain Dumbass turned and left, Specialist Fox said not to pay any attention to him, as he was a dumbass. I laughed. I left and went up to the third floor to check it out. When I got there, I was face-to-face with one very big and mean-looking MP. He had to be over six feet tall and two hundred fifty pounds or more. He asked who I was and what my business was, and I said I was driving for General Collins and I was just checking the place out. He asked if I had a security clearance and I told him no. He said no one was allowed on the third floor without a clearance and not to come back without one. Being a general's driver was no help this time. That was the one and only time I was on the third floor.

I left to go back outside. I had never seen so many commissioned officers in my life: lieutenants, captains, majors, lieutenant colonels, and full colonels. If the place got a bomb dropped on it, half the officers in Vietnam would have been taken out—and maybe one driver. I walked out of the cool air-conditioned building into the hot mid-morning heat of Vietnam, where a friend of mine was using one of those duster cloth rags with a short pole on his car. There were no car washes, and long water hoses were hard to come by. Sometimes during the monsoon season, we would get a bucket full of soap and wash the cars in the rain. You had to be fast though because the rain would stop as fast as it started. It was like someone turning a faucet on and off.

The guy dusting off his car had a small transistor radio sitting on top of the car playing some rock 'n' roll music while he tried to dance and dust at the same time. It was a sight to see. I can't recall the guy's name, and that's what hurts sometimes. You spend a year in a war zone together and go through some tough things only you and he will ever know about. Yet I can never remember names. I can always remember their faces and facial expressions, though.

At five minutes till noon, Specialist E-7 Fox called me on the walkie-talkie and told me to pull the general's car in front of the building because he would be on his way out at any minute. As I got the car pulled up in front of the building and the back door open, General Collins and the two captains came out. I was standing at attention and gave the general a salute.

He asked if I was hungry and I said, "Yes, sir, I am."

"Let's go eat," he said.

I found out later from Captain Morse that Captain Dumbass was a little jealous of me because of the way the general would shoot the breeze with me—as I was only a lowly specialist in his eyes. After the general got in, Captain Dumbass got in the back on the other side and Captain Morse got in the front seat beside me. Captain Dumbass always rode in the back because he had one month more time-in-grade than did Captain Morse.

We pulled out of the compound heading north on Beach Road until we reached the road running in front of the villa. After everyone had gotten out of the car, Captain Morse said to go around to the back of the villa and the cook would give me something to eat. I went around to the back and went inside to where drivers ate their meals. The generals sat around a big table in another room with their food brought to them, like a restaurant. The cooks here were either specialist E-6 or specialist E-7. After chow, I went back out to the car where Captain Morse was having a cigarette. So I had one too. We discussed the high cost of a pack of cigarettes, $0.10 a pack. We agreed that if they ever got to $0.15 a pack, we would give them up. They are $4 to $5 a pack nowadays.

At 1:30 pm we headed back to the Headquarters Compound. The general almost always took an hour and a half for lunch. After parking the car, I went up to ask Specialist Fox if he had anything for me to do. He told me no, I should just take it easy until around 6:00 pm, when the general would be going back to the villa. What a job. I even got paid for it, too. I knew I should not do it, but I walked over to the NCO Club for a cold beer. The place was locked up, which happened to be good for me because Specialist Fox called on the walkie-talkie and said the general would be going to the airport at any time. I hardly had time to pull the car around before the general and the two captains came out. The general was flying to Saigon for an unexpected last-minute meeting with General Westmoreland, the commander of all the U.S. Forces in South Vietnam.

After leaving the airport, I went by my old company to see Tim, but some FNG said he was on a convoy.

As I was leaving I heard someone call out, "How you been getting along?"

I turned around to see the first sergeant with a big smile on his face.

Jokingly, he said, "I figured you would be a sergeant by now, being the general's driver and all."

We talked for a while until he said he had to get back to work, unlike some people who drove for generals. We both laughed, and he said to come back and visit whenever I could. I went back to the Headquarters Compound to talk with Specialist Fox while waiting for the general to return. Specialist Fox was sitting at his desk doing some typing, but he stopped when I came in and offered me a cold drink of tea. We talked for a while and I found out that he had been in the Army for seventeen years. He also said that General Collins is the fourth general he had worked for in his Army career. He said General Collins was the best to work for. We talked for about two hours until he got the call saying the general would be arriving back at the airport in about thirty minutes and would be going straight to the villa for the rest of the day.

After picking up the general and the captains, we drove to the villa and then I was off until the next morning. Not bad for the first day, I told myself. What a job to have in the middle of a war zone. On my second day of driving for General Collins, a funny thing happened. About 10:00 am, a major general I had never seen before up close was leaving the compound as I was cleaning out my car. Just before noon, Specialist Fox had called and said the general was on his way down. I had just pulled the general's car in front of the building and opened the rear door—I could see General Collins standing in the hallway talking to someone—when the major general's car pulled up behind mine. The correct procedure would have been for me to pull my car up a ways so his car was in front of the building. I could see General Collins, though, and I was expecting him to come out at any second. Well, I guess the major general got tired of waiting on me to move my car so he got out of his car and came over to me with his back to the building. He didn't know I was driving for General Collins. I stood at attention and gave him a salute without getting one in return.

He said: "Didn't you see the two stars on my car? How come you didn't move this car? Who are you driving for?"

He was really beginning to chew me out, his voice getting louder to where everyone could hear him. The whole time I could see General Collins standing in the doorway listening to the major general. About this time, General Collins walked up and asked what the problem was. I was still standing at attention with the salute waiting on him to return it. When an enlisted person gives an officer a salute, you are to hold it until the officer returns it. The major general turned around and saw General Collins and came to attention himself.

He said, "I didn't know this was your car and driver."

General Collins said: "If you had given my driver the opportunity to answer, you would have found that out. Do you think it's time to return a salute to my driver?"

After giving me a salute, he resumed his salute to General Collins. General Collins said that would be all for now but to be in his office when he returned from lunch.

The major general said, "Yes, sir."

Nothing else was said to me about the occurrence. This was one of those times that being a driver for the general paid off.

General Collins wasn't feeling good on Friday and stayed at the villa on Saturday and Sunday, so my time driving for him was cut to five days. On Saturday morning, a doctor was called to the villa, and he told the general to stay in bed because he had a virus. Being a general had its rewards. On Monday morning, I went to the Headquarters Office to give the walkie-talkie back to Specialist Fox. As I was about to leave, General Collins came out of his office to give Specialist Fox some papers and then turned to me and said that I had done a fine job driving him. He smiled and told me to watch out for those two-star generals. General Collins was a very good and decent man. I had a lot of respect for him. He had a lot of responsibility, but he would take the time to say something nice to a lowly enlistee like myself.

One day as we were leaving the Headquarters Compound, after only going about twenty feet, an FNG private, about eighteen or nineteen years old, walked out right in front of us like he had no idea what was going on. What he should have done was stop and come to attention and given a salute until we passed by. After I hit the brakes hard to avoid running into the guy, Captain Morse jumped out of the car and went over to the guy to say something to him. Before he could say anything, General Collins called for the private to come over to him. I was thinking the guy was going to get his butt chewed out by a three-star general.

Instead, General Collins said: "Soldier, don't you know you could have gotten run over walking out in front of a car like that? Now get along and be more careful."

The guy was shaking and looked like he had just seen a ghost. That's the kind of person I saw the general to be.

I was back driving for the majors, colonels, and VIPs. The next-to-last week of June, the first sergeant called me into his office and said I was to report to Specialist Fox as soon as possible. The first sergeant said I was to be the permanent driver for General Collins. He said he had no idea why except that the general had asked for me personally. I left and went to see Specialist Fox. He said that I was to go and get all my gear because I would be living at the villa, and that my only job would be to keep the general's car clean and be the general's driver. I asked Specialist Fox what had happened to the other driver, and he said that the driver had been caught trying to smuggle drugs back into Vietnam from his R&R. I left to go get my gear and returned to the villa and loaded into the small room used by the other driver. The room was ten foot by ten foot and private. I had it all to myself.

It was Sunday, so I took the time to clean the place because it was filthy, dirt everywhere. I got all of my stuff put away, and I was thinking how lucky I was. My own room, driving for a three-star general, and only about two more months left to go in Vietnam. The last thing I had to do was to put my short-timers' calendar on the wall.

CHAPTER 31

July 1970

On the first of July, I woke with sixty-three days and a wake-up to go in Vietnam. The wake-up means waking up on your last day in Vietnam. It would turn out to be a particularly good day for me, but more about that later. The next morning at precisely 7:00 am, General Collins came out of the villa, like he did most mornings, but this morning was different. He was not wearing his uniform, instead wearing a swimming suit with a towel tossed over his shoulder. It really was a funny sight to see. I could hardly keep from laughing because I was not expecting to see a three-star general in a swimming suit in the middle of a war zone at 7:00 am in the morning. The general got in the car and said to find a good spot at the beach. The two captains were in a state of shock, as was I, because we had no idea he was wanting to go for a swim. The MP escort didn't see the general come out in his swimsuit because they were parked outside and behind the five-foot brick wall in front of the villa. They had no idea we were heading for the beach.

We pulled out of the villa and turned right onto Beach Road. The general said to pull off the road at the first opportunity I got. I pulled off the road and drove as far as I could without getting stuck in the sand. The general got out of the car and walked down to the water. The two MPs came over to me laughing, and said that if they knew we were going to the beach they would have brought their suits, too. The general swam for about thirty minutes and then we went back to the villa so the general could shower. Then we headed to the Headquarters Compound. Not your usual day in a war zone.

The next morning the general went to the Headquarters Compound until 10:00 am and then I took him to the air base. He and the two captains were going to be gone until later that day. I had a few hours to kill, so I went to see my old friend, Tim.

I walked into the hooch and Tim was writing to someone, and I said, "I didn't know you could write."

He looked up with a big smile and said, "Attention, the general's driver is here."

For the next three hours we sat and talked and got caught up on everything. Tim said they had just gotten back from a ten-truck convoy.

On their convoy, he said, they had gone up north to deliver some supplies to five different outposts in the middle of nowhere. He said those guys were some of the filthiest people he had ever seen. He said they had not taken a bath for over a month because they could not get any water delivered to them. They were really happy to see them because they had two water trucks filled with water. On their way back to Nha Trang, one of their trucks had engine trouble. He said while the mechanic was working on the engine, they began to receive sniper fire and mortar rounds. All the guys were firing in the direction of the snipers. The gunships came in and took care of the snipers while they got the truck fixed, then they got the hell out of there. Two of their guys got hit, one in the arm and the other in the leg. They would be receiving Purple Hearts. They both were new guys who had been in-country for less than a month.

Tim said the place was not the same without Sam, Moose, and me around. He said some of the guys were dumber than dirt. Around this time, Specialist Fox called me on the walkie-talkie and said the general would be arriving at the air base in thirty minutes. I said my goodbyes to Tim and left. We promised to get together again soon. After picking up the general and the captains, we went straight to the villa and I was off duty for the day. The cooks had one-inch-thick steaks prepared for our meal that night, with apple pie and ice cream for dessert. I went back for a second helping of ice cream. What a job. Just another day as a REMF. We almost always got to eat what the generals were eating. That night after we had eaten our meal, I went to my room to write some letters. It was so hot that my sweat was dripping onto the paper.

I went and got two cold beers and walked out to the front gate where an MP was on guard duty. Some nights when there was nothing else to do, I would just go out and visit with them for a while. The guards were not supposed to drink while on duty, but they did sometimes anyways. On this night, I knew the guy would take it. I got to know the MPs pretty well, and we got along just fine.

Near the end of July, I was the only one at the villa after returning from taking the general to the air base when all of a sudden I could hear a lot of small-arms fire nearby. My first thought was that we were being attacked by VC. I grabbed my M-16 and ran inside the villa and up the stairs that led to the roof so I could get a better view of what was going on. The roof was flat like most of the other villas, and I could see all around the area. I could see the MPs at the front gate coming and going with a look of fear on their faces. There was an awareness of danger in the air. Then I could hear a few more rounds going off in the direction of the MP company down the street.

A half-hour went by with no more shots, so I went down and walked over to the front gate and asked the MPs what was going on. They said one of their men, a big black PFC, had walked into the MP Company Office and shot and killed the commanding officer and the first sergeant because he was supposed to have left Vietnam last week. The first sergeant and CO didn't like him because he was always getting into some kind of trouble, so they kept him in Vietnam as long as they could as a form of punishment. I knew the guy. He was big and very friendly to me. Whenever he had escort duty for the general, we would talk about going home and he would always tell me what a gravy job I had. Whenever he pulled guard duty on the front gate of the villa, I would always bring him a cold beer and he would always try to pay me for it. A few days later I heard he was taken to the prison at Leavenworth, Kansas, where he would probably spend the remainder of his life.

Tim came to the villa one evening to visit and see if I would like to go to the NCO Club for a beer. He said he had heard that a pretty good Filipino band was going to be playing there. We got to the club as the band walked on stage. They were made up of two guys and two very pretty girls. The girls did all of the singing while the guys played the instruments. They were the best band I had heard up until that time. They played a lot of the rock 'n' roll songs popular with the GIs at the time. They played "Light My Fire" by the Doors, "Black Is Black," "Coming to Take You Away," and the Beatles' "Hey Jude." They also did a good job with "Purple Haze" by Jimi Hendrix. But the song that got all the GIs fired up was "We Gotta Get Out of This Place" by the Animals. After drinking more beers than we should have, we left the club and went back to Tim's hooch. Some of the men were sitting outside and watching the fireworks hitting the mountain north of Nha Trang. This night, the gunships were really putting a lot of rounds into the mountain.

The first sergeant came out of his hooch to watch the fireworks, too, but I didn't know it until I heard someone say, "Okie, what are you doing in my company area?"

We talked for a while, and then as I was getting ready to leave he said to be careful because there were reports of the VC in the area. He said that's why the mountain was getting lit up. He also said that he had recommended me for promotion to sergeant. He said that I was deserving of it and that Okies had to stick together. After telling Tim we would get together soon again, I headed back to the villa.

On the way back, I could see the artillery rounds hitting the side of the mountain. They were really lighting the area up. Just as I got to the villa and out of the car, the alert signal went off. For the rest of the night, you could hear the gunships and the artillery rounds pounding the area in and around the mountain. I grabbed my M-16 and a few beers and went up to the roof of the villa to get a good view of the fireworks. To my surprise, Captain Morse was there drinking a beer and watching the artillery hit the mountain too. I asked him what he thought about Captain Dumbass. (His real name was Captain Hall.) He said that he did not like him as a person but that they had to work together so he tried to get along with him. He said that he disapproved of the way he treated the enlisted men. I asked him what he thought of General Collins next. He said that he was a very nice person and a good man to work for.

The fireworks show on the mountain was letting up. I asked Captain Morse about the reports of VC in the area, and he said the VC were always in the area. But this time, just after sundown, the Fifth Special Forces had been out on a patrol and came across a large unit of VC camping at the base of the mountain, where they were now firing. It was just past midnight and the all-clear signal went off, so we decided to turn in for the night. It was still hot at this time of night, and I had a hard time falling asleep. But before I knew it, the sun was coming up and it was time for another day in Vietnam.

I walked out to the car and waited on the general to come out, as it was almost 7:00 am. Captain Morse was already there and talking to the two MPs sitting in their Jeep. Captain Dumbass came out without saying a thing and then went over to the car and walked around it. He then turned to me and said I needed to get the car cleaned up. I looked over to Captain Morse and he was shaking his head. Captain Morse told me later that the car looked just fine to him. That's the way Captain Hall, or Captain Dumbass, was always talking to the enlisted men.

At 7:00 am sharp, the general came out of the villa and got in the car. I turned the key but nothing happened. The car battery was dead. My first thought was, *Oh shit, now what am I going to do?*

General Collins said, "Driver, do you know how to pop the clutch if we get behind the car and give it a push?"

I told him I knew how. So the general and the two captains got out of the car and started to push the car. After going about twenty or twenty-five feet, I let out the clutch and the car started. As I said before, the MPs were behind the five-foot wall in front of the villa, so they had no idea what was going on when my car came out from the other side of the wall with the general and captains pushing. They had the funniest, most unbelieving looks on their faces watching the officers push the car.

After getting inside the car, General Collins said to take the car to the motor pool and get a new battery in it after I dropped them off at the Headquarters Building. I wish I had a picture of the general pushing me in the car. They say a picture is worth a thousand words. I arrived at the motor pool, where a staff sergeant was sitting behind a desk and reading a *Stars and Stripes* newspaper.

Without looking up, the staff sergeant says, "What can I do for you?"

I told him that I needed a new battery for my car because the current one was dead. He looked up and said that it would be about two hours because all the men were busy.

I said: "Staff sergeant, I am the driver of General Collins, and I need a new battery now because I need to get back to headquarters and take the general to the air base in an hour."

The staff sergeant looked at me with a smirk on his face and said: "Specialist, it will be two hours. I don't give a damn who you drive for."

I got on the walkie-talkie and told Specialist Fox what the staff sergeant said about not giving a damn who I drove for. Specialist Fox said to put the guy on the walkie-talkie.

I gave it to him and said, "It's for you."

After saying "yes, sir" about a dozen times, the staff sergeant gave me the walkie-talkie and jumped up from his desk and left. In about five minutes I heard someone outside. I looked out and the staff sergeant was putting a new battery in my car. He came back in and said that I was ready to go. He was sweating and out of breath.

I left and got back to Headquarters and asked Specialist Fox what he said to the staff sergeant that made him jump up so fast and replace the battery.

He said, "I told him I was his commanding general and if my driver was not back here in the next thirty minutes, he would be demoted in rank and transferred to an infantry unit by the next day."

Just then the phone rang and it was the staff sergeant asking if I had made it back in time. Specialist Fox and I had a good laugh over that. After that event, I would always have the car running before the general got in.

The general was getting ready to leave, so I went and pulled the car around and left it running. The general got in and asked if I had any trouble getting the battery.

I said, "No, sir, no trouble at all."

After arriving at the air base, I pulled up next to the plane like I always do to let the general out. On this day, I was in for a big surprise.

As I pulled up next to the plane, the general said to me, "Driver, park the car and come with us."

I was in shock. Here I was, just a specialist E-4, and I was going to get to fly on a three-star general's jet plane. You should have seen the look on Captain Dumbass's face. He was in a state of disbelief.

After parking the car and getting on the plane, we took off. I had no idea where we were going. On the plane were a pilot, co-pilot, the general, the two captains, and me. The plane had seats for twelve people. Looking out the small window at the jungle below, I was thinking how lucky and blessed I was. I was thankful that I was not in infantry and walking through the jungle below like my brother Carl had done. I was thankful that I was no longer going on convoys, not knowing what was waiting up the road or around the bend. I was thinking how lucky I was to be the driver for a three-star general and getting to fly on his plane. At the same time, though, I was feeling a little ashamed because so many others had it a lot worse. I was thinking that when I got back home, would I be able to tell anyone how easy my last two months in a war zone were for me—or if should just keep it to myself? Then I thought, someone had to do it, why not me? I looked over at Captain Morse, and with a big smile on his face, he gave me two thumbs up as if to say, "Everything is good."

We arrived at Long Binh Post, which was about fifteen miles northeast of Saigon. Long Binh was a gigantic military complex, the largest U.S. military area in the world. The Long Binh Complex consisted of the huge Long Binh Post and numerous other attached compounds making up a sprawling city of tens of thousands of people: buildings of all descriptions, including large World War II–style barracks like the ones they still used on U.S. military bases. There were interspersed paved roads, storage depots, vehicle parks, and heli-pads spread out over square miles of red dirt. Very little vegetation could be found. Swirling red dust was everywhere in the dry season, and the place was a sea of mud during the rainy season. The complex overflowed with the amenities associated with military bases worldwide. It had PXs filled to the brim with the latest technology and toys, stereo shops, dozens of movie theaters showing first-run movies, recreation centers, libraries, swimming pools, and clubs for officers, NCOs, and enlisted men. There were Chinese restaurants with incredibly low prices. In a fleet of air-conditioned trailers, there was a full mini-college campus for off-duty personnel. There were several graduate programs available, a junior college, a technical school, and remedial programs.

Long Binh Post even had its own government-franchised bordello. I thought I had it made at Nha Trang. Long Binh Post was truly a REMF citadel. These guys probably spent their entire year on this base before going home and then told the folks how bad they had it in Vietnam. It had been just over two hours since the general had entered the building for their meeting, and I had no idea what it was about. It was way above my pay grade. The meeting was finally over and we flew back to Nha Trang. As we got off the plane, one of the MPs had driven the car up to the plane because I always left the keys in the car.

As the general walked up to the door to get in, I gave him a salute and said, "Thank you, sir, for letting me go on the plane with you."

With a smile he said, "Did you enjoy yourself?"

I told him I sure did. We left and drove to the villa and I was off duty for the day.

For chow that night, I had one of the best-tasting steaks I've ever had. What a day. It's a day that I've always remembered, even after all this time.

CHAPTER
32

August 1970

The first of August, I woke up with thirty-two days and a wake-up to go left in the Republic of South Vietnam. It began as most every other day, but that night would be a lot different than other nights. After I took the general to Headquarters and parked the car, Specialist Fox called me on the walkie-talkie and asked me to come up and see him. Specialist Fox was a very nice person and always treated me with respect. He said my former first sergeant had called him and recommended me for sergeant E-5. He said I would be going in front of the promotion board next week. I asked him about the promotion board, and he said it mostly was made up of a first sergeant, a captain, and a major. They would each ask a question or two about anything. He said it may help to study up on world affairs and learn all I could about the war we were currently in. I asked if the general would be going anywhere and if I could go pick up a few things from the PX. Specialist Fox said he had no plans for the day.

I offered to get Specialist Fox whatever he needed, but he said he had already been to the PX just the day before. About this time, Captain Dumbass came out of his office and said he had a list of things for me to get at the PX as soon as possible. I didn't mind going to the PX for him. I just wished he had asked instead of telling me. Captain Morse came out of his office about that time, too, and so I asked him if he would like anything. He told me no, but thanked me for offering. After returning from the PX, Captain Dumbass was talking to Specialist Fox so I walked over and gave the captain the bag of stuff I picked up for him at the PX. Without saying a word, he turned and walked into his office with his goodies.

It was almost chow time, so I left to go pull the general's car around. After returning to Headquarters and letting the general out, I noticed one of the tires was almost flat. I got the spare out of the trunk but it was also half-flat. I called Specialist Fox and said I was going to the motor pool to get the tires fixed, and he told me if I had any trouble with the motor pool sergeant to let him know. I arrived at the motor pool just in time because the tire had gone completely flat by then. I walked into the motor pool office and the staff sergeant was sitting behind his desk reading another *Stars and Stripes* newspaper.

As soon as he saw me, he jumped up from his desk and said: "Hello, Specialist Lott, what can I do for you?"

I told him I had a flat tire and he said he would get it taken care of right away. He left and returned in about an hour with four new tires on the car. He said to put in a good word for him to the general.

I got back to the office and told Specialist Fox what the staff sergeant did and what he said. Specialist Fox gave the staff sergeant a call.

The staff sergeant answered the phone, and Specialist Fox said: "This is General Collin's office. The general would like to thank you and the motor pool personnel for taking care of the general's car."

A few days later, I saw the staff sergeant at the NCO Club and he bought me a beer. We sat and talked for a while and he turned out to be a very nice person. After taking the general to the villa that night and then eating chow, all the drivers, cooks, and other helpers were invited to watch a movie.

The villa had a very large room that was turned into a movie theater for the officers and generals. This would be my one and only time to watch a movie at the villa. The movie that night was "Patton," with George C. Scott in the leading role. It was about the World War II hero General George S. Patton. It was a very good movie, or at least I thought so. Over the years, I have watched the movie many times, and every time, I think back to that night in 1970 in the middle of a war zone, sitting in an air-conditioned building watching it for the first time. I was sitting with three generals—a brigadier general (one star), a major general (two stars), and a lieutenant general (three stars). We were all watching a movie about a general, while eating popcorn the cooks had popped for everyone. What a night to remember. While watching the movie and getting caught up in it, you couldn't tell a war was going on around us outside. Stepping outside after the movie and hearing the artillery rounds hit the mountain took you back to reality, though.

The second week of August, I had twenty-five days left in the Republic of South Vietnam. On Monday morning at 10:00 am, I arrived at the building where the promotion board would be held. There were seven of us going up for sergeant but only five openings available. As we were sitting outside waiting on our names to be called, I looked up and saw Tim walking up to me, a big smile on his face. He asked if my name had been called yet. I was surprised and had no idea Tim was up for sergeant, too.

I asked him, "How come you didn't tell me?"

He said that he just found out yesterday from the first sergeant after he got back from a convoy.

My name was finally called, and as I walked in, to my surprise, my former first sergeant, the Okie, was on the promotion board. As I looked over at him, he had this big smile on his face. I was very nervous because making sergeant was a big deal, and it would mean a bigger paycheck. I was so nervous that the only question I currently remember was from the Okie first sergeant.

He asked me, "Why are we in Vietnam?"

Ever since I joined the Army, I had heard of South Vietnam falling to communist North Vietnam, and if that were to happen, then all of Southeast Asia would fall.

I said: "First sergeant, the American military is in South Vietnam to keep the communist North Vietnam from taking over Southeast Asia. It's the 'Domino Theory.' If America did not help South Vietnam and let it fall to the rule of North Vietnam, then one by one every nation in Indochina would be overthrown by communists. It would be a terrible outcome for the free world to accept."

When my interview was over, I went outside as Tim's name was called out. I waited for him and thought how nice it would be for us both to make sergeant. Tim finally came out, and I could tell he was just as nervous as I was. I asked him how it went, and he said that he thought it went well. I told him the same. By this time, it was almost time for chow, and I had to get the car pulled around for the general and Tim had to get back and get ready for guard duty for that night. We said if we both made sergeant then we would get together and have a party. If not, we would still get together and have a party.

That night after chow, around 8:00 pm, Captain Dumbass called me up to the room that he and Captain Morse were sharing. Captain Morse asked me how the interview had gone. I told him that it went well and that I was hoping I made sergeant.

He told me: "Don't worry. I'm sure you did just fine and you'll be wearing sergeant's stripes before too long."

Captain Dumbass came walking into the room carrying a .45-caliber pistol.

He hands the pistol to me and said, "I need you to take this gun and clean it and bring it back tonight."

I looked over at Captain Morse and he had this funny expression on his face, like he couldn't believe what he had just heard. I turned and walked out into the hallway and stopped. I was thinking what a real ass the captain was. He was either too lazy to clean his own weapon or he just had to show his authority, once again.

The more I thought about it, the madder I got. I was thinking that I needed someone to talk to and I knew just who that someone was. The very moment I knocked on the general's door, I began to think, *This may not had been a good idea.* Perhaps I should have thought it out more. I still had time to run away, but then the door opened and there I was, standing there with a .45-caliber pistol.

The general had this look of surprise and shock on his face and said, "What can I do for you, Specialist Lott?"

I said, "Sir, I'm sorry to disturb you, but I would like to talk to you about something."

He said: "No problem at all. Come in and let's talk about it."

We sat at a small table with a few books on it, and the general asked me if I liked to read. I told him I did. He asked what books I preferred reading and then asked how the interview for sergeant had gone. He also asked how many more days I had left in Vietnam. I guess he could tell I was nervous so he was making small talk trying to calm me down.

After what seemed like a long time, but only ten minutes in reality, he said, "Now, Specialist Lott, what can I do for you?"

I said: "Sir, I'm sorry to have interrupted your evening. Perhaps I should go and figure this out for myself."

He said, "You're already here, so let's try to figure it out together."

I said: "Sir, it's Captain Hall. I'm not trying to get him into any kind of trouble, but he is always having me run all his errands for him and he never asks. He's always telling me to do it, without ever saying thank you. Now, I do run errands for Captain Morse, but he always asks and always tells me thank you. But the real reason I'm here is because Captain Hall called me up to his room about half an hour ago and gave me his pistol. He told me to clean it and to bring it back to him by tonight. I believe each soldier should be responsible for his own weapon, even more so in a war zone. I'm not trying to disobey Captain Hall. I'm just standing up to something I disagree with."

The general said, to my surprise: "I agree with you. Each soldier is and should be obligated to take care of his own weapon whether in a war zone or not."

He told me to leave the weapon with him and not to worry about Captain Hall. He said if I have any problem in the future, I could come and talk to him about it at any time.

As I was leaving the general's quarters, I was thinking how everything seemed to have gone well. The general could have said to do as I was told, or he could have said never to disturb him again, or he could have even had me court-martialed. The more I thought about what could have been, the more I needed a beer.

The next morning as I was waiting for the general to come out of the villa, Captain Morse came out and lit a cigarette and walked over to me with a grin on his face.

He said: "I don't know what you did last night, but Captain Hall was called to the general's quarters and he came back with a very red face and his pistol. I could tell he was mad, but when I asked him about it, he said that he didn't care to talk about it."

I told Captain Morse about going to General Collins' quarters and telling him how I felt about having to clean someone else's weapon. Captain Morse said he understood, but taking my problem to a three-star general takes a lot of nerve to stand up for something that I believed in. He also said, with a laugh, that it took a big set of balls.

General Collins and Captain Dumbass came out and we left for the Headquarters Building. From that day on, until I left Vietnam, Captain Hall did his best to not say a word to me, which was just fine with me.

The third week of August, I was outside waiting on the general to come out and figuring my time left in Vietnam. It was eighteen more days. I remember it was a very hot morning that day, and I was thinking how nice a day at the beach would be. I also remember thinking that it would be a perfect day to get my orders for promotion to sergeant.

Captain Morse came out of the villa and walked up to me and said, "The general would like to see you right away."

He asked if I had gotten into any trouble, and I assured him that I hadn't. I walked into the villa, and all the cooks, drivers, and General Collins were standing there.

I walked up to General Collins and gave him a salute and said, "Specialist Lott reporting to the general, sir."

General Collins said, "Sergeant Lott, you are out of uniform."

It didn't dawn on me that the general said "sergeant" until he reached over and took off my specialist E-4 insignia and replaced them with an E-5 sergeant insignia.

He then said: "You are now in the right uniform, Sergeant Lott, congratulations. Now we need to go to Headquarters."

After arriving at the Headquarters Building and parking the car, I got out and lit a cigarette, wondering if Tim had made sergeant also.

I then heard someone say, "Sergeant," but I didn't pay any attention to it.

Then I heard: "Excuse me, sergeant, I just arrived here last night. Can you tell me where the Mess Hall is at?"

Being called a sergeant was going to take some getting used to. After showing the PFC where the Mess Hall was, he asked how long I had been in Vietnam.

I said: "Too long. I have eighteen days to go."

He said he'd been here for four days. He said he just got here after being in Cam Ranh Bay. I wished him good luck and went to see Specialist Fox to show off my new sergeant stripes.

I walked in to the office and Specialist Fox said, "Congratulations, sergeant."

I asked if the general would be going anywhere, because if he wasn't I wanted to go find out if my friend had made sergeant. He said the general had no plans to leave the office, but tomorrow after lunch, the general would be flying to Saigon for a meeting with General Westmoreland and would be staying overnight.

I left and drove over to see Tim. As I arrived, Tim was coming out of the first sergeant's office.

I walked over to him and we both said at the same time, "How's it going, sergeant?"

Tim had just received his sergeant's stripes. We said that we had to get together and celebrate. I told him tomorrow night would be good because the general would be in Saigon for the night. Tim said that would work too because the first sergeant approved a three-day pass for him. I told him I had to get back but that I would be back tomorrow evening. Before I left, I walked into the first sergeant's office to say hello.

When he saw me he said, "How you doing, Sergeant Okie?"

I told him I was just dropping by to say hello and thanked him for helping me make sergeant.

He said: "You did all the work. I just put you in for it."

He asked if I had talked to Tim yet, and I told him that I had and that we planned on getting together the following evening to celebrate.

I said, "If you come by, I'll buy you a beer or two."

He said he might have to take me up on that. Then he asked if I knew who my replacement would be yet, and I said that I don't think anyone had been chosen. He asked if I thought Tim would like the job and if I thought he would do a good job at it. I said that I thought he would be a fine driver for General Collins. He asked me not to say anything to Tim until he got to talk to Specialist Fox about it. I assured him I would not say a word.

After leaving, I stopped at the on-base Vietnamese barbershop to get a haircut. As I was walking in, the motor pool staff sergeant was coming out. He noticed my sergeant stripes and asked when I got the promotion. I told him about five hours ago. He said he was going up for sergeant first class E-7 next week. Then he said the general's new car would be ready tomorrow. It was the first time I had heard about getting a new car.

After getting the haircut, I went back to ask Specialist Fox about getting a new car. He said that he had just heard about it himself just an hour before, and that he had no idea who had authorized it. Then Specialist Fox asked me about Tim. He said we need to find a driver for the general in the next few days so I could show him and tell him what is expected of him. He said the first sergeant had called and recommended Sergeant Baker (Tim) and asked if we were good friends. I said that we were, and that Tim was a very smart, intelligent, and resourceful person. I said he had just gotten his sergeant stripes this morning, like myself. I told him that I was sure he would do a fine job as the general's driver. Specialist Fox was worth his weight in gold to the general. The officers might give the orders, but the enlisted men got it all done. The office belonged to Specialist Fox. He made all the appointments, arranged all the meetings, did all the typing and just about anything else that needed to be done. To see the general, you had to go through him first. Nobody gave him any trouble. He was somewhat like me. Working for the general had its benefits.

After chow that night, I got some beer and went and sat on top of the villa because it was hot. Up there, you could catch a breeze from time to time. Every so often an artillery round would hit the side of the mountain. It was a good place to do some thinking. Here I was, a sergeant for almost a day. I had been in the Army for only twenty-eight months, and I already made sergeant. It usually took a lot of guys three or four years to do it. I knew a few guys back in Germany who had been in for six years before they made sergeant. I was thinking if I made a career out of the Army and stayed in for twenty years, I should be at least a sergeant first class E-7 and would retire at the age of thirty-eight years old. That meant I would have seventeen years to go. This was 1970, and 1988 seemed like an eternity away. After all, I was only twenty-one, and to most young men, seventeen years is a long, long time. If only you could look ahead into the future.

Around this time, the artillery guys began putting a lot of rounds into the mountain back behind the west of Nha Trang. They must have gotten reports that VC were in the area. Or they were having target practice on behalf of the U.S. government. The next day after taking the captains and General Collins to the air base for their overnight stay in Saigon, I was on my way to the motor pool to see about the new car. As I arrived, the staff sergeant was just parking the new car. I pulled up alongside it. The staff sergeant said that it was ready to go. After getting my stuff and personal things out of the old car and into the new car, I was on my way back to show it to Specialist Fox. I looked at the odometer and it only had twenty-seven miles on it. This was a brand-new 1970 Chevrolet automatic, and it even had air conditioning in it. I turned on the air conditioning, thinking I was in heaven. It got cold in no time.

When the staff sergeant said "new car," I thought he was talking about one that was a year or so newer than the 1966 Chevy I was driving. I was thinking, nobody back home would believe me if I told them I was driving a brand-new 1970 Chevy with air conditioning in the middle of a war zone. I could hardly believe it myself. God is good, I thought.

After returning to Headquarters and parking the car, I gave Specialist Fox a call on the walkie-talkie and told him about the car. He said he would be right down to take a look at it. By the time he arrived, a lot of people were around the car checking it out. Specialist Fox arrived and we got in the car and I turned on the air conditioning. He could hardly believe it was brand new.

We got out, and with a laugh he said, "Was green the only color they had?"

Specialist Fox had to get back up to the office because someone had to be there twenty-four hours a day in case of any emergency conditions requiring prompt action. Specialist Fox hardly left the office because he had a small room across the hall for his living quarters. He laughingly said one time that he was never late for work. I told him I was going to go see Sergeant Baker, and we were going to celebrate our promotions. He told me to keep the walkie-talkie close by just in case.

It was late in the afternoon when I arrived at Tim's hooch. We were soon off to the NCO Club. On the way there, Tim was amazed at the new car and particularly the air conditioning. I asked how he would like to have my job, and he said he would love to have it.

"Who wouldn't love it," he said.

We got to the NCO Club and the Okie first sergeant was already there. We walked over to his table and he said to have a seat, addressing us by our new ranks. After we had a few beers, the first sergeant asked Tim if he would like to be put in for driving for General Collins. Tim said that he would kill for the job.

The first sergeant said, "Good, because on Monday morning you are to be interviewed for it by Specialist Fox."

Tim could hardly believe it. He said the next beer was on him. The first sergeant said it was time for him to get back to the company. We had already had six or seven beers by then, so I asked Tim if he was ready to get back to his hooch. He obliged and said he had just gotten some marijuana in that he would like for us to try.

I asked the first sergeant if he would like a ride in a brand-new car.

He said, "Yes, but I get to sit in the back."

On the way there, about a dozen or so men we passed gave us a salute because only officers rode in cars. They couldn't tell a first sergeant was sitting in the back seat. The first sergeant was feeling no pain after all the beer. Walking our way on the side of the road was a PFC without a ball cap on his head.

The first sergeant said, "Let's have some fun with this guy."

He said to pull over next to him, and when I did, he rolled down his window and said: "Solider, you are out of uniform. Where is your head cover?"

The guy said, "In my pocket, sir."

The first sergeant said: "Son, do I look like an officer? I am a first sergeant. I work for a living, and if I ever catch you without your ball cap on again, I'll send your young ass off to infantry."

The guy said: "Yes, sir. I mean, yes, sergeant."

We arrived at the first sergeant's office and after getting out of the car, he said, "I had a good time and we should do it again sometime."

Tim and I went back to his hooch. He got the weed and rolled a cigarette. We put on some rock 'n' roll music, had a beer, and lit up the joint. We were both feeling good. Not only because of the beer and weed, but because of making sergeant, Tim becoming the general's driver, and me having just a couple weeks left in Vietnam. Tim got up to get another beer and fell down. I went over to help him but he had passed out, so I carried him to his cot, out like a light. He never could hold his beer very well.

It was now nearly 10:00 pm, so I decided to go back to the villa to my own cot and get some sleep since the party was over. As I got into the car, I was thinking if I should try to drive as high and drunk as I was. As I began to pull the car onto Beach Road, Specialist Fox called on the walkie-talkie and said that the general was not staying overnight, and that he would be landing at the air base in about forty-five minutes. My first thought was, *I can't drive in this condition.* The general would know that I'm high, and what if I ran the car off the road or ran into someone. It would be very bad to get promoted and then demoted in the same week. I arrived at the air base and got out of the car as the MP escorts did, too. I went over to say hello to them, and they asked if I had been drinking since I was walking a little funny.

I said, "Yes, I just came from a party."

They asked why the general was returning tonight, and I said that I had no idea—it was above my E-5 pay grade.

The general finally arrived after another hour and a half. It was good for me because it gave me more time to get rid of the high I was on and to sober up some more. After picking up the captains and the general, we headed for the villa. Somewhere along the way, the general asked me how I liked the new car.

I said, "Just fine, sir, but it would look better in red."

No one said a word so I guess they didn't think it was funny. We arrived at the villa and General Collins and Captain Dumbass went inside. Captain Morse did not. He asked if I had been drinking and smoking weed. I told him yes because I was not expecting them back until tomorrow. I told him my good friend and I were celebrating our sergeant promotions.

He asked laughingly, "Did you save any weed for me?"

I asked if he could still smell it on me, and he said there was a slight odor but only because he was the one sitting next to me. I asked if he thought the general had smelled it, and he said he didn't think so because if he had he would have said something because the general did not like his soldiers using marijuana. I was thinking, once again, how lucky I was. No more beer or weed for me.

On the last day of August, my countdown was down to a week left in Vietnam. I woke up thinking how short I was. As the saying went, I was so short I could sit on a dime without my feet touching the ground. After I arrived at the Headquarters Building and parked the car, Tim came over to me and said he was ready for his interview. He went up to the office and I introduced him to Specialist Fox. Specialist Fox said he needed to talk to me when the interview was over, so I went down to the front desk to talk to some of the MPs on duty.

After half an hour, Tim came down, and I asked how the interview had gone and he said, "You are looking at the new, soon-to-be driver for Lieutenant General Collins."

Tim said that Specialist Fox had told him to go get his personal belongings and to take them to the villa and find a room since he would start driving for him in the morning.

I said: "Tomorrow morning? I still have a week to go."

I asked Tim to wait on me until I could talk to Specialist Fox and see what was going on.

I went up to the office and Specialist Fox said to have a seat because he had good news for me. He said my orders had arrived and I had received a five-day drop. Instead of leaving on September 7th, I would be leaving on the second. He said I had one day and a wake-up to go. He told me the general had no plans to go anywhere, so I could go help Sergeant Baker get moved into the villa. I left and went to tell Tim what was going on. He was as excited as I was. He was excited about moving into the villa, and I was excited about going home five days early. As we got back to Tim's hooch to pack up his belongings, First Sergeant Okie came walking out. He said that Specialist Fox had just called him about Tim moving to the villa. We talked for a while, and he said he hated to see both of us leaving. He said that we both did a fine job for him and that we were fine soldiers. I told him I had just received my orders this morning about being able to leave Wednesday. We said our goodbyes, and after getting Tim's belongings in the car, we were off to the villa to find him a room.

After arriving at the villa, we found a room about half the size of mine. Tim said it was just fine for a few days because he would just move into mine after I left. It was getting close to chow time, so I left Tim to unpack while I returned to Headquarters to pick up the general. After taking the general back to the office after chow, I had a few errands to run. I got my dental and medical records and made sure all of my shots were up-to-date. I then went to the Finance Office to get my financial records. I went back to Headquarters to pick up the general and went back to the villa.

On the way to the villa, the general said, "I see you will be leaving us soon."

I said: "Yes, sir. Wednesday will be my last day in Vietnam."

He asked me about Tim and said, "I understand you and Sergeant Baker are good friends."

I said: "Yes, sir. We are very good friends, and starting tomorrow, Sergeant Baker will be your new driver."

We arrived at the villa and I went to go find Tim. He was sitting on his cot reading some mail from home.

He looked up and said: "This place is nice. I didn't realize how good you had it here."

By then, it was time for chow. After introducing Tim to everyone and eating, we got some beers and I took Tim to my get-away place on the rooftop. I told him that this is where I went to be alone and to think most nights. I told him no one ever came up here except for Captain Morse to have a beer with me. I also told him that when the artillery guys are firing at the mountain, that this was the place to be. Tim asked if there was anything I could tell him about the job that he should know. I said there were two very important things to remember. First, never be late in picking up the general. Second, always have the walkie-talkie with you at all times. Whether you are at the PX, getting a haircut, or going to the latrine, always have the walkie-talkie with you so that Specialist Fox can get ahold of you twenty-four hours a day. I also reminded him to never smoke weed anytime he was on duty. We talked for some time about going home, about Vietnam, and about the first time we had met. We talked a lot about Moose and of all the good times the three of us had together. We talked about all the convoys we had gone on and how lucky we were to still have all of our body parts.

We finally turned in around midnight.

CHAPTER 33

September 1970

The next morning, September first, I woke up with only one more night to go in Vietnam. It was almost 7:00 am, so I went to see if Tim was up. His room was empty so I went around to the side of the villa where the car was parked and there he was, standing with the back door open and waiting on the general. He looked up and saw me, so I gave him a thumbs-up. After getting a cup of coffee, I returned to my room to start packing my personal stuff up. After getting everything ready and throwing away stuff I no longer needed, I decided to give the place a good cleaning. I didn't want to leave a dirty room for Tim. The rest of the day went by very slowly for me. Around 10:00 am, I thought I would go to the NCO Club for a beer since I had nothing else to do. I walked around to the car and then remembered I no longer had a car. Instead, I got a few beers and went up to the top of the villa. Around noon, Tim pulled the car in front of the villa with the general for chow. I went down and asked how things were going.

He said: "Great. I'm really liking the job so far."

That afternoon went by very slowly for me because of the anticipation of going home the next day. After eating chow that night, I was called into the large room used for showing movies. I had no idea why. The other drivers, cooks, Captain Morse, Captain Dumbass, and General Collins were there.

General Collins was standing up front, so I walked up to him, stood at attention, and said, "Sergeant Lott reporting to the general, sir."

He began by saying what a fine driver I was and what a fine job I had done, and then he said, "I have some awards for you."

I had been awarded the National Defense Service Medal, the Vietnam Service Medal, the Vietnam Campaign Medal, the Good Conduct Medal, and the Army Commendation Medal, which was signed by General Collins. A few other awards were given to other men, also.

I returned to my room and Tim came in carrying two beers.

He said, "I sure do hate to see you leave because it won't be the same without you."

He congratulated me on my awards, and I told him I was glad I didn't receive the Purple Heart, and Tim said, "That's one I can live without, too."

We stayed up past midnight again just talking and drinking beer. I looked over at Tim and once again he was passed out. He still couldn't hold his beer. I carried him to his cot and tried to sleep myself, but I had no luck because all that was on my mind was the following day.

The next morning, September second, the sun was coming up on my last day in South Vietnam. I said a thank you to God for keeping me safe for the past year. As it was getting close to the general coming out of the villa, I walked around to the front and Captain Morse was talking to Tim. He came over to me and I gave him one last salute, and after he returned it, he reached out his hand and we shook. He wished me a good life. I asked Tim if I could open the door for General Collins one last time. He had no problem with it. As the general came out, I was standing with the door, at attention holding a salute.

Without returning my salute, he reached his hand out and as we shook hands, he said, "Sergeant Lott, it has been nice knowing you and I wish you the best of luck."

Tim returned to the villa after dropping off the general and gave me a ride to the air base. We arrived there just in time. The chopper was leaving within ten minutes for Cam Ranh Bay—the same place where I landed in-country one year before. We barely had time to say goodbye. We wished each other luck and gave each other a quick hug and handshake.

It was another hot day, but with the air flowing through the chopper, it made the ride a lot better. This was a smart pilot. Instead of flying out over the jungle, he flew along the coastline where it was a lot safer from any sniper fire. This would be my last ride on a chopper, and I would never forget it since it was taking me out of Vietnam. We arrived at the airstrip at Cam Ranh Bay. I got off the chopper and walked across the hot tarmac to the Aircraft Hangar Building to check in for my flight home. There was a group of other soldiers doing the same thing. The sergeant on duty was checking everyone's orders and medical records, looking at our shot records to see if everything was up-to-date. There were some men who had to get shots before they could leave Vietnam. He said the next flight out would be leaving in about an hour, and not to miss it or we would be staying in Vietnam for another day. No one dared to wander off.

In the heat of the middle of the day, my "Freedom Bird," which is what every soldier called the plane going back to the States, landed. The passengers exited. Most of them were FNGs, and some were soldiers returning after their week of R&R in Hawaii. My group met them in single file as we walked across the hot tarmac to board the plane. We boarded as quickly as we could. I took a seat and put on the headset provided with various music channels. As the plane began to taxi for takeoff, that song by the Animals, "We Gotta Get Out of This Place," began to play. How fitting. I choked up and cried a little. I was crying for thanks. I was so thankful to be a "survivor" of Vietnam. I was thankful to my God that I was not wounded or had to leave behind any of my limbs in Vietnam. I was thankful to be going home alive, unlike the thousands of young men and women who did not.

After I got home from Vietnam, Tim and I stayed in touch for a while, but in time, we just stopped writing to each other. I got on with my life, and I guess he did the same. I remember the last letter I got from him. He said that General Collins was being transferred to somewhere in Europe. He also said he heard something about the general asking him to go and continue being his driver. Both Tim and General Collins got to Vietnam in January of 1970. Tim said he didn't know if he would go if asked, because it would not be until January of 1971. That was the last I heard from him.

Tim, if you are reading this, give me a call.

Epilogue

In January 1973, the signing of the Paris Peace Accords marked an end to U.S. military involvement in South Vietnam. There were more than 58,000 Americans known to have been killed in Vietnam. It was a terrible cost of American lives. There are two historical points I cannot forget—one being April 30, 1975, and the other January 1977. The city of Saigon fell to the communist government of North Vietnam on April 30, 1975. While watching the events unfold on television, I began to think of my brother Carl, my good friend Moose, and all the other men and women who were killed and wounded. I had to ask, "Why?" Why did my government abandon the Vietnamese people?

In January 1977, on his first full day in office as the president of the United States, Jimmy Carter, in his first action as president, proclaimed a full and complete pardon and amnesty to all men who had failed to submit to the draft and had hidden during the war in Vietnam either on United States soil, in Canada, or elsewhere. His giving this group a pardon was a slap in the face to all Vietnam veterans. When I heard the news of the pardon, I became sick to my stomach and had an ache in my heart. I fought back tears for the 58,000 American men and women who had given up their lives and died on Vietnamese soil. The anger I felt towards the government in its disregard for the blood, sweat, tears, and sacrifices of both life and limbs—and mental well-being—of Vietnam veterans is still with me today. I realized that the only way other Vietnam vets and I can ever "heal" is to tell others about Vietnam and the price paid in sacrifices by those of us who were ground forces in that place synonymous with Hell.

* * *

The first week of March, 2017, my wife and I were at a Home Depot store looking at some things when a Vietnamese girl, maybe around thirty years old, came up to us and asked if she could help us with anything. She was an employee there. When she saw the ball cap I was wearing with "Vietnam" across the front, she

Paul with his Vietnam hat on in 2018

asked when was I there and where I was stationed. She said her family was from Saigon. We talked for a while, and then she asked if she could give me a hug.

As she gave me a hug, she said with tears in her eyes, "Thank you for fighting for my country."

It's been forty-seven years since I left Vietnam, and this is the first time anyone gave me a hug and said "thank you." That someone just happened to be Vietnamese, too.

Someone asked me when I was last in Vietnam and I said, "Last night."

I left Vietnam, but Vietnam has never left me.

Made in the USA
Monee, IL
28 February 2025

SURGEON GENERAL'S WARNING: Garage Sales Can Be Habit Forming And Cause Sleepless Saturday Mornings, Pre-Sale Anxiety, And May Add To House Clutter And Flat Wallets.